The Expert Guide to PeopleSoft Security

The Expert Guide to PeopleSoft Security

Jason D. Carter, MS

iUniverse, Inc.
New York Lincoln Shanghai

The Expert Guide to PeopleSoft Security

iUniverse, Inc.

For information address:
iUniverse, Inc.
2021 Pine Lake Road, Suite 100
Lincoln, NE 68512
www.iuniverse.com

ISBN: 0-595-32440-1 (pbk)
ISBN: 0-595-66579-9 (cloth)

Printed in the United States of America

Legal Stuff

This book is dedicated to my family, my wife Kelly and my two boys, Kent and Evan. Without their support and patience this book would never have been completed. Yes, boys, now Dad can play computer games again.

Contents

CHAPTER 1   Basic Security Design 1

CHAPTER 2   User Profile Setup 4

CHAPTER 3   Role Setup 9

CHAPTER 4   Permission List Setup 13

CHAPTER 5   Process Security 28

CHAPTER 6   Query Access Manager 31

CHAPTER 7   Row Level Security 35

CHAPTER 8   Portal Structure 41

CHAPTER 9   Security Migration & Back-Up 52

CHAPTER 10   Definition Security 55

CHAPTER 11   LDAP Authentication 59

CHAPTER 12   Base User Profiles 70

CHAPTER 13   Password Controls 72

CHAPTER 14   Creating Dynamic Roles 76

APPENDIX A   PS 8.1 Security Tables 79

APPENDIX B   PS 8.4 Security Tables 83

APPENDIX C   Useful Security Queries 89

APPENDIX D   Authorized Actions Codes on PSAUTHITEM 97

APPENDIX E   Special PeopleSoft Roles 99

1

Basic Security Design

Before we begin, there a few basic concepts you need to be familiar with in order to understand PeopleSoft Security.

Login Validation

It is important to remember that users log into the PeopleSoft system itself and that the Application Server controls this login. Users do not login to the database directly nor do they have any database specific permissions or a user id on the database itself. PeopleSoft maintains its own 'metadata' tables, such as PSOPRDEFN that hold basic user and password information. When a user makes a data change in the system, the appserver writes this change to the actual underlying database table using an Access ID that has rights on a 'sysadm' database level. While each user is connected to an Access ID, it is done so by an intermediary Symbolic ID that is in turn connected to the Access ID. This greatly limits the number of people needing to know the actual username of the Access ID on the database as well as its password.

So when a user logs in, there is a call by the appserver to the database to, 1) check that the user is valid and, 2) to check the password (this can work differently if you are using LDAP or Single Sign On). Once the user is validated, the appserver itself speaks to the database on the user's behalf using the Access ID. This is important because if you are trying to audit a data change it must be done within PeopleSoft itself, because the Access ID will perform every action on the database itself.

Menus, Components & Pages

It is important to understand the basic concept of how PeopleSoft pages are developed in terms of Menu & Component structures. Let's start at the back-end.

A Page is assigned to a Component group that may contain multiple pages, and in this relationship the actions available for any particular Page are also defined (Add, Update/Display, Update/Display All and Correction). Next each Component is assigned to a Menu Group. This relationship was a lot more apparent in the menu structure before the use of the Portal in 8.4, where now any component can be placed pretty much wherever you please in terms of PIA navigation.

The best way to determine which Menu, Component and Page you are on in the system is to use 'Control-J' key combination. This brings up a web page with the relevant details of the page you are working on.

Permission Lists, Roles and User Profiles

Just as important as understanding how Menus, Pages and Components are developed, is comprehending how they are secured. Again we will start from the back and work our way forward.

Permission Lists are the basic building block of PeopleSoft Security. Ultimately all page access is defined on a Permission List level. The Permission List contains (among other things we will look at later) pages and their access options. For instance, if you created a new page called, *MyPage*, You would add the page to a Permission List with specifications for its access (Add, Update/Display, etc...). Don't worry about those specifics yet (that's what Chapter 2 is for), but know that the Page is connected to a Permission List.

Next, the Permission List is assigned to a Role. The Role for the most part, is simply a structure that "holds" one or more Permission Lists. So lets say you assigned the *MyPage* page to a Permission List called *MyPermissionList* (I sense a theme...). You would then assign *MyPermissionList* to a Role, such as *MyRole*. Remember that the Role can contain multiple Permission Lists.

Finally you would then assign your Role to a User Profile. The User Profile is the actual "account" for a user in PeopleSoft. In addition to identification related information, the User Profile is also attached to Roles. So for instance if you attached *MyRole* your User Profile, you would finally have access to *MyPage* because:

MyPage is assigned to *MyPermissionList*.
MyPermissionList is assigned to *MyRole*.
And finally, *MyRole* is assigned to your User Profile.

And so begins our adventure in the land of PeopleSoft Security.

2

User Profile Setup

User Profiles and other basic security objects (such as Roles and Permission Lists) are not built on Effective Dated records, as are many other objects within PeopleSoft. This means that all changes made are immediate (barring some caching issues, but in theory 'immediate'). There is only one row per user in the PSOPRDEFN table, which is the base record where user data is maintained. To access User Profiles navigate to *PeopleTools-> Security-> User Profiles-> User Profiles* in 8.4 and above, or to *PeopleTools-> Maintain Security-> Use-> User Profiles* in earlier releases.

General

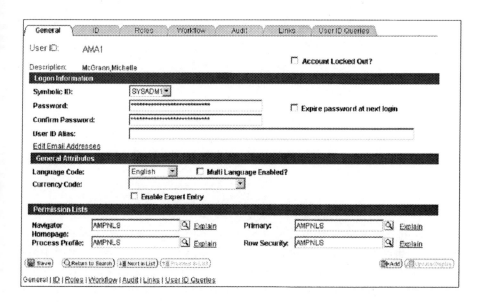

This page holds the basic user information. The Symbolic ID is a "key" that points to the Access ID and its encrypted password in the database. This page also allows you to set Language Codes, Currency Codes, Lock Accounts (effective the next time they login; current sessions will continue uninterrupted) and Expire & set passwords. This page also allows you to set Primary Permission Lists, which are discussed next.

Permission Lists

The permission list section allows you to define settings for individual users that are derived from settings related to a specific permission list. While most settings on a permission list are cumulative, meaning that you get everything from everyone you are assigned to through a role, these settings are a one for one deal. For instance, on the Process tab of a Permission List are Process Profile Permissions. These permissions define server options, override certain server options, define the process requests you can view and so forth. Even though these are defined on a Permission List, each user only has one specific set of these types of permissions, so they are assigned to the User Profile itself by means of a Permission List.

Navigator Homepage

PeopleSoft determines a user's Navigator Homepage by looking at the Navigator Homepage attribute of the Navigator Homepage Permission List. This setting is related to workflow.

Process Profile

PeopleSoft determines a user's Process Profile by looking at the Process Profile of the Process Profile Permission List. This controls user options related to *how* processes are run, not *which* processes can be run. These details are found on the Process Profile Permissions link on the Process tab of a Permission List.

Primary

PeopleSoft determines Row Level Security by using settings associated with both the Primary and Row Security Permission Lists. In general these Permission Lists are used to control the actual data within a table that can be accessed by a particular user based on an attribute such as Department, Business Unit or Setid. The specifics of what is controlled and how varies from Application to Application, so you should consult the documentation for your particular module to be clear on the details.

In addition to Row Level Security, the Primary Permission List also controls access and options related to Mass Change, PeopleTools and Definition Security.

Row Security

PeopleSoft determines Row Level Security by using settings associated with both the Primary and Row Security Permission Lists. In general these Permission Lists are used to control the actual data within a table that can be accessed by a particular user based on an attribute such as Department, Business Unit or Setid. The specifics of what is controlled and how varies from Application to Application, so you should consult the documentation for your particular module to be clear on the details.

Row Security is most often used to determine department-based security in HR.

ID

The ID Page allows you to enter unique identification information about the user. First an ID type is selected (Employee, Customer, etc...) and then this brings up a field to enter in the ID itself. If there is no ID stored in the system (such as a Finance Database with no corresponding HR data in production) you must choose the ID type of 'None'.

 If any ID type other than 'None' is selected without a corresponding ID attribute, such as an Employee ID, you will not be able to save the User Profile.

Roles

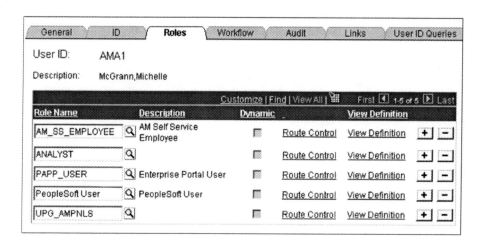

Roles are added to the User Profile to give cumulative access to various pages, pieces and parts within PeopleSoft. On each row in 8.4 and above, you can select the View Definition link to take you directly into the Role Definition itself, an extremely convenient feature when troubleshooting.

Workflow

This page allows you to set basic workflow information, including Supervisor ID, Alternate user, and an option to reassign all workflow entries. This page includes a version of effective dated logic allowing you to specify from and to dates for the period of time during which you want workflow directed to an alternate user, such as during a vacation.

Audit

This page displays information concerning the last change made to this user profile row on the PSOPRDEFN table. It tells you the time and User ID associated with the last change. This option only shows the very last change, so if you suspect something was changed erroneously and really need to see who did it, be sure to look before you change it back and save.

Links

Allows you define custom links to other parts of the security system for convenience.

User ID Queries

This page provides useful, predefined online queries to give you quick information about your user profiles. Please note that this query is only available in PeopleTools 8.4 and above.

3

Role Setup

Roles are the intermediary step between Permission Lists and User profiles. They allow groupings of Permission Lists, usually based on a user's job role, which are then assigned to User Profiles. The Roles also provide groups that are used by workflow for various routings as well.

To access Roles in 8.4 and above navigate to *PeopleTools-> Security-> Permissions & Roles-> Roles*, or *PeopleTools-> Maintain Security-> Use-> Roles* for earlier releases.

General

Contains basic description information about the Role, and provides an option to disable the Role.

Permission Lists

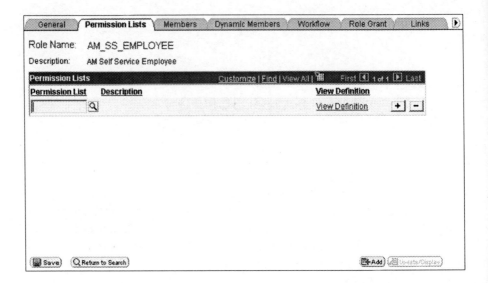

This is the page where Permission Lists are assigned to the Role. Like the Role assignments on the User Profile, the permissions granted are cumulative (with the exception of certain options such as Process Profile information, which are assigned to user profiles via the Permission lists on the General page of the user profile). Again, there is a View Definition link on each row that will allow you to go to the permission list shown in Tools 8.4 and above.

Members

This page gives a view of all the User Profiles who have this Role assigned to them. This is only a view. You cannot assign Users to the Role directly. The Role instead, must be added to the User Profile.

Dynamic Members

Roles can be assigned to users dynamically by use of various rules. These rules can be built using Query, PeopleCode or in conjunction with an outside Directory. This has traditionally been most useful when dealing with work-flow related issues, but has potential when dealing with Users contained within Directories that have enough identification data to define a role such as a Manager of a particular department.

Workflow

This page contains basic workflow options such as allowing notifications, recipient lookups and the option to user queries for the routing of workflow.

Role Grant

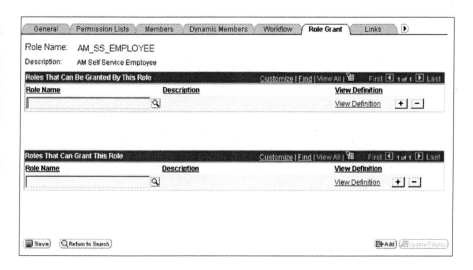

This page allows you to set-up functionality needed to use Distributed User Administration. On this page you can define Roles which members of this Role are allowed to assign to other users. You can also view and assign Roles that can grant the current Role you are working in. This allows users of a 'Distributed Administration' role to assign particular roles in their areas to other users, allowing this task to be taken off the plate of the traditional security administrator.

Links

Like in User Profiles this allows customized links to other pages for the sake of convenience to the administrator.

Role Queries

Gives access to convenient, predefined, online queries regarding your Roles. This feature is available only in Tools 8.4 and above.

Audit

This page works the same as the Audit Page for User Profiles. Again you only get the last User and Time associated with the latest change to the row.

4

Permission List Setup

Permission Lists are the ultimate heart of PeopleSoft Security. This is where the nitty-gritty of page access is granted as well as many other security options. Permission Lists are then assigned to Roles, which are then assigned to Users. You cannot give page access to a user directly.

To access Roles in 8.4 and above, navigate to *PeopleTools-> Security-> Permissions & Roles-> Permission Lists*, or *PeopleTools-> Maintain Security-> Use-> Permission Lists* in earlier releases.

General

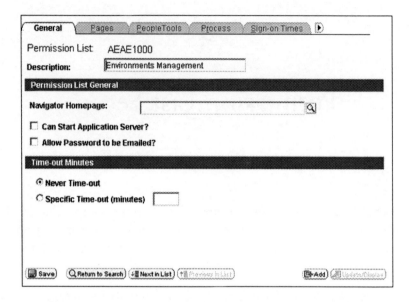

The General Page not only gives descriptive information, but it also allows you to set some very important options.

You can set a Navigator Homepage here, but remember that the Navigator Homepage setting on the Primary Permission List section on the General Page of the User Profile controls this option.

This page also allows you to set a permission list to give permission to a User ID to start an Application Server. This allows that ID to be used in the settings (PSAPPSRV.CFG) for the Application Server as the login used to start the Application server itself.

User Time-out minutes can also be set by permission list here. There are also global time-out limits that are set on the web-server and Application servers, so keep in mind that the shortest time out limit will win (even one from another permission list the user is assign to via a role), so this requires a higher level of coordination if you wish to set time-outs at the permission lists level.

Pages

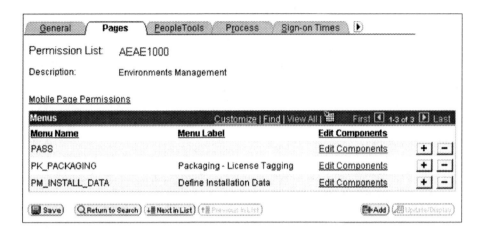

This is where you assign page access, but it is a little more involved than just that. On the first page here you add a menu (remembering that the menu contains components, which in turn contain the actual pages). Once you add the needed menu, you then click on Edit Components to see the components in the menu.

Component Permissions

Manage Cash

Components	Customize | Find |	First ◀ 1-19 of 19 ▶ Last		Select All
Authorized? **Component Name**	**Item Label**	**Edit Pages**	**View Content References for this Component**	**Deselect All**
☑ POS_GENERIC_ENTRY	Manual Position Entry	Edit Pages	View	
☑ CASH_POS	Position Manager	Edit Pages	View	
☑ FEE_GENERATOR	Fee Entry	Edit Pages	View	
☑ TR_TRANSFER_COMP	Funds Transfer	Edit Pages	View	
☑ BANK_TRANSFER	Bank Account Transfer	Edit Pages	View	
☑ TR_WIRE_PNLG	EFT Request Entry	Edit Pages	View	
☑ POS_REPORT_PERIOD	Report Periods	Edit Pages	View	
☑ TR_INT_ACU_RC	Calculate Interest Accruals	Edit Pages	View	
☑ POS_MGR_SCHED	Schedule Position Manager	Edit Pages	View	
☑ MESSAGE_LOG	Message Log	Edit Pages	View	
☑ BNK_INT_ACCT_BAL	Internal Account Activity	Edit Pages	View	
☑ COMP_SRCH_RSLT_COM	Component Search Results	Edit Pages	View	
☑ TR_GEN_NAV	Cash Management Home	Edit Pages	View	

This page shows you the list of Components, which the developer associated with the menu. Notice that all the check boxes are grayed out. You cannot simply click on a component to add it or remove it. You can click Select All or Deselect All that will globally select full permissions to every page of every component listed or globally remove all the access. To select page access individually within a component (which will usually be the case) you click the Edit Pages link on the row for the Component.

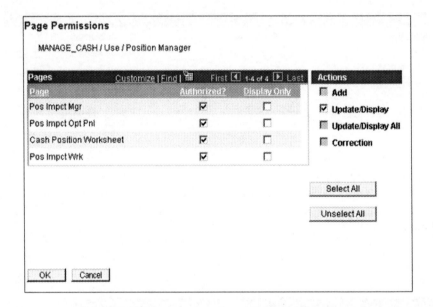

This is the actual location where you select specific permissions for your pages. First you can select whether users have access to the page at all by choosing the corresponding check box under the Authorized column. If you with them to have only read access to a page you simply select the Display Only option. Next you will see a list of Actions associated with every page in this component object.

- Add: Allows the user to add a new row of data on these pages.

- Update/Display: Allows the user to Update and Display the current, effective dated row of data.

- Update/Display All: Allows the user to Update all Current and Future effective dated rows of data and Display all Past, Current and Future dated row.

- Correction: Allows users to Change all rows of data including Past effective dated rows, basically changing history. This should only be given if absolutely necessary.

Notice that not all the Action choices are available on all components. The developer at the component level defines available actions.

 Please Note *To quickly find out the actual Page Name, Component and Menu for a particular page, navigate to that page in the system and press the Ctrl-J Key combination to bring up this information.*

PeopleTools

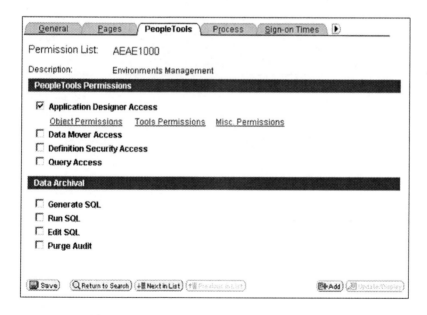

Most of the PeopleTools Permission options are fairly straightforward; simply check the box for access. The sub-permissions for the Application Designer

Access are a little more involved though and must be set in addition to the 'check box' access.

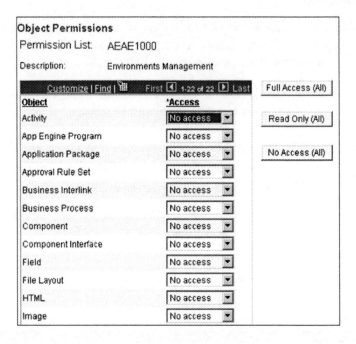

Each PeopleSoft Object that can be accessed in Application Designer must have permissions explicitly granted. Each object for the most part can have 'Full', 'Read Only' or 'No Access' assigned to it. You can also click the buttons on the page to globally set them all.

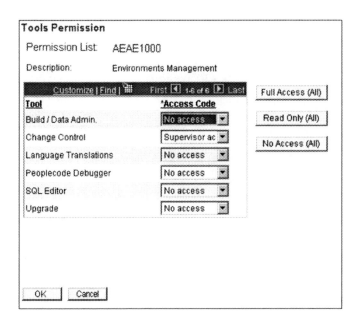

Tools permissions set access to other tools associated with development. Build/Data Admin is the most powerful one because it allows a developer to Build out and Alter tables on the database. This is dangerous in itself even in a development database, but if done incorrectly in Production, it can wipe out all the data in a particular table. This permission should be highly limited and closely controlled.

Process

The Process page has two sets of associated permissions, Process Group Permissions and Process Profile Permissions.

Process Group Permissions

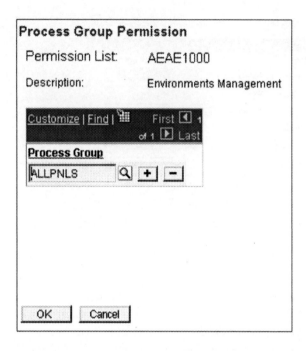

Process group permissions explicitly define which Process Groups a Permission List has access to run. The Process Groups themselves are defined as part of the Process Definitions which will be looked at later.

Process Profile Permissions

```
Process Profile Permission

  Permission List:     AEAE1000

  Description:          Environments Management

  ┌─ Server Destinations ──────────┐    ┌─ Allow Requestor To ───────────┐
  │                                 │    │                                 │
  │  File:  %%OutputDirectory%%      │    │  □ Override Output Destination  │
  │                                 │    │                                 │
  │  Printer: lpt1                   │    │  □ Override Server Parameters    │
  └─────────────────────────────────┘    │                                 │
  ┌─ OS/390 Job Controls ──────────┐    │  □ View Server Status            │
  │                                 │    │                                 │
  │  Name:  [        ]               │    │  □ Update Server Status          │
  │                                 │    │                                 │
  │  Acct:  [          ]             │    │  □ Enable Recurrence Selection   │
  └─────────────────────────────────┘    └─────────────────────────────────┘
  ┌─ Allow Process Request ────────┐
  │                                 │
  │  *View By:   None  ▼             │
  │                                 │
  │  *Update By: None  ▼             │
  └─────────────────────────────────┘

  [ OK ]   [ Cancel ]
```

The process profile is assigned directly to the user via the Process Profile Option on the Permission Lists section of the General Page of the User Profile. Settings such as File and Printer must be present for many processes to successfully. The 'Allow Requestor To' has some very important choices as well that deal with what the user con control when running a process, such as overriding the run parameters or scheduling recurrences of a process to run automatically. The View By and Update By options will default to Owner, but you may wish to set View By to All to allow others to see the details of the process run and check to see if scheduled processes have completed successfully or not.

Sign-on Times

Sign on times are fairly straightforward and default to 24/7 access. They are setup by adding each day of the week and explicitly defining the hours and minutes of access. Remember that these setting are cumulative based on permission lists assigned to roles and then to users. To use them effectively, permission lists need to be set up specifically for the purpose of hours access (such as one for weekday 9-5 access, one for Week-end access, one for 24/7 etc...) and then the sign-on times information must be effectively removed from all other permission lists. Not a simple task to make them work correctly.

Component Interfaces

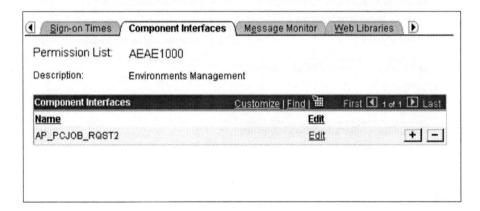

Components can have interfaces built for them that allow programmatic access from inside or outside of PeopleSoft to their pages and underlying records. When adding access to the Interfaces, be sure to hit the Edit button and explicitly set the allowed methods as shown below. By default there will be No Access on all methods until they are specifically set as in the screen-shot below.

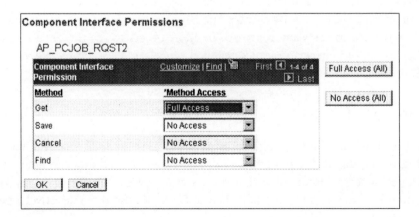

Please Note *One Component Interface that is very important but often overlooked is the USERMAINT_SELF Interface. This provides access allowing a User to maintain their password. Without proper settings here they will not be able to change their password even if they can access the correct page.*

Message Monitor

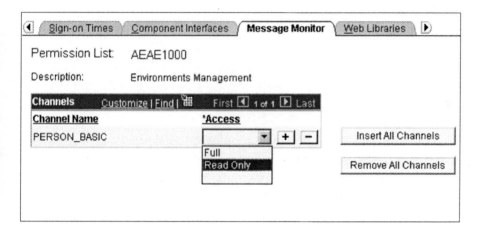

This page allows administrators access to view the data flowing between PeopleSoft Databases via Integration Broker. This data is broken into Channels and access is defined here to allow administrators to view the channels and related messages on the Message Monitor component of the Integration Broker. Read only access won't cause harm but full access can allow messages to be restarted and channels to be paused (among other things) and can cause problems, so only give it to those who need it.

Web Libraries

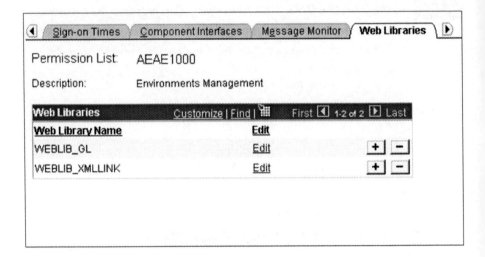

Web Libraries are needed to access various web portal pages and functionality. A base user profile (basically a role and permission list created to be shared by a large number of user providing basic, necessary security), generally ties back to a permission list with Web Library settings allowing users to see the portal itself. The Options shown above are needed to allow users to run an Excel Import of Journals into GL. Again you must add the Web Library and then click Edit to explicitly define access, otherwise the default will be No Access, and after you save and return to the permission list you will not even see the Library name anymore.

Personalizations

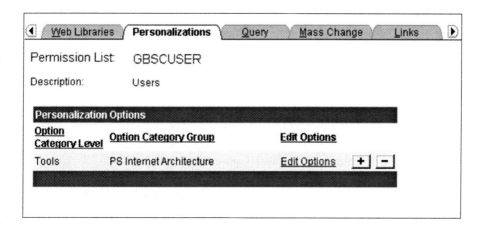

The Personalizations tab controls users access to customize certain personalization options within the system, via the *My Personalizations* link on the root menu. Generally the most important of these are the Tools—PS Internet Architecture options, which are shown below.

Personalization Permissions			
Option Category Level:	PeopleTools		
Option Category Group:	PS Internet Architecture		

Personalization Options			
Category	**User Option**	**Description**	**Allow User Option**
General Options	ACCESS	Accessibility Features	☑
Interntl & Regional Settings	ADES	Afternoon designator (PM, pm)	☑
Navigation Personalizations	AUTOMENU	Automatic menu collapse	☑
Navigation Personalizations	CALBTN	Tab over Calendar Button	☑
Interntl & Regional Settings	DCSP	Decimal Separator	☐
Interntl & Regional Settings	DFRMT	Date Format	☑
Interntl & Regional Settings	DTSP	Date Separator	☐
Navigation Personalizations	EXPERT	Default Expert Entry On	☐
Navigation Personalizations	GRDRWS	Max rows for View All	☐
Navigation Personalizations	GRDTAB	Tab over Grid Tabs	☑
Navigation Personalizations	HDRICN	Tab over Header Icons	☑
Navigation Personalizations	LKPBTN	Tab over Lookup Button	☑
Interntl & Regional Settings	LTZONE	Local Time Zone	☑
Interntl & Regional Settings	MDES	Morning designator (AM, am)	☑
General Options	METAXP	Time page held in cache	☑
General Options	MLTLNG	Multi Language Entry	☑
Navigation Personalizations	NBAR	Tab over Navigation Bar	☑

Please Note *Be particularly cautious when setting these options and avoid a blanket use of the Select All button. Notice for instance in the above example that the Save Warning option would allow users to turn off the save warning feature, which of course can be problematic for users.*

Query

Query access is granted in a cumulative manner from a combination of all permission lists associated with a user. This makes adding query access simple enough, but to remove access you may have to do a lot of backtracking to find everywhere a particular access group is assigned. It is probably a good idea to create permission lists that do nothing but control various levels of Query access, and avoid placing these settings in other Permission Lists.

Access Group Permissions

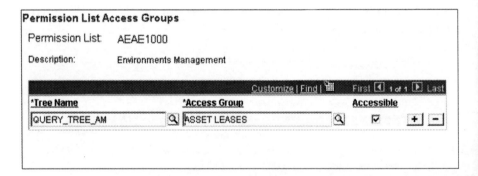

Access Groups control the tables that a user can see and query against while using PeopleSoft's Query tool. The table must first be a part of an Access Group and then the Access Group must be assigned to a Permission List that the user's roles have access to. Notice here that Access Groups themselves are created as part of a Query Tree and must be added in that context, by first picking the Tree and then the Access Group.

The building of Access Groups and Query Trees is discussed Chapter 6.

Query Profile

```
Permission List:    AEAE1000

Description:        Environments Management

┌─ PeopleSoft Query Use ─────────────┐   ┌─ Advanced SQL Options ──────────────┐
    ☐  Only Allowed to run Queries          ☑  Allow use of Distinct
    ☑  Allow creation of Public Queries     ☐  Allow use of 'Any Join'
    ☐  Allow creation of Workflow Queries   ☑  Allow use of Subquery/Exists
                                            ☑  Allow use of Union
    Maximum Rows Fetched:     [ 1000 ]      ☐  Allow use of Expressions
    (0 = Unlimited)
                                        Maximum Joins Allowed:        [    ]
┌─ PeopleSoft Query Output ──────────┐  (9 = Unlimited)
    ☑  Run
    ☑  Run to Excel                     Maximum 'In Tree' Criteria:   [    ]
    ☐  Run to Crystal                   (9 = Unlimited)


   [  OK  ]    [ Cancel ]
```

The Query Profile controls what a user can do in terms of the Query tool.

The PeopleSoft Query Use section controls how a user can use queries, such as only being able to run queries, but not create or modify them. You can also control the ability to create Public Queries and Workflow queries by selecting the appropriate options here.

The PeopleSoft Query Output section controls how you can output queries. Basically you can run a query online, run it into Excel or run it into a Crystal report, based on what privileges you are granted here.

The Advanced SQL Options section allows you to control the functionality a user is granted when creating queries. Due to system limitations or concerns about potential system performance issues, you may want to limit the number of joins allowed in a query, or limit someone's ability to use the Distinct clause. If you are not familiar with SQL based query functionality you will probably want to consult your DBA when setting up these options, in order to assess any potential performance issues.

5

Process Security

The Process Scheduler

The Process Scheduler allows users to run Batch Processes online through PIA. These processes can be run immediately or scheduled for a later time. This is also how PeopleSoft runs reports such as Crystal and SQR, so end-users' access to the Process Monitor and Process Groups are highly important.

Process Monitor Access

Access to the Process Monitor itself is given by granting access to the PRO-CESSMONITOR component on the PROCESSMONITOR menu as discussed earlier (in the Permission Lists section). This basic access will allow users to view the progress and details concerning processes that they themselves have submitted.

At times certain users will need the ability to view processes submitted by others. To grant this ability, PeopleSoft delivers a Role called ProcessSchedulerAdmin. This role works in conjunction with PeopleCode in the application itself and therefore contains no Permission Lists. PeopleCode within the Process Monitor Component checks whether or not a user is assigned to this Role and if they are grants them the ability to see all Process requests regardless of who submitted them.

Please Note   *Be aware that the ProcessSchedulerAdmin Role is all or nothing. You can grant a user access to everyone's Process Requests or only their own. There is no way to grant access based on individual users or groups of users.*

Process Definition Options

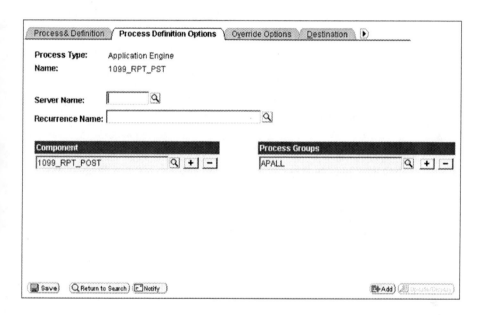

Access to run Processes themselves is controlled via Process Groups. Unlike other PS objects that require set-up in another area before they can be used, Process groups are created right here. Simply entering a new name in the Process Group section of the Process Definitions Options Tab found on the Processes Component, creates a new group. To navigate to this page go to *PeopleTools-> Process Scheduler-> Processes* in 8.4 and *PeopleTools-> Process Scheduler Manager-> Use-> Process Definitions* in earlier releases. Delivered Processes are already associated with delivered Process Groups, such APALL, etc...and new Processes can be added to these groups as well. To give access to a Process, you add one of its related Process Groups to a Permission List, on the Process Tab under the Process Group Permissions link described in the Permission List Section.

It is highly advisable that you click the search button when selecting a Process Group to add a Process to. This field is Case-sensitive and if you were to enter "Apall" instead of "APALL", you will have inadvertently created a new Process Group which is not attached to a Permission List in the system.

Here is an example:

Let's say that a developer has created a new Application Engine Process called MY_PROCESS. He has already associated it with the APALL process group, but you wish to create a new group for it called CUSTOM.

1. Navigate to PeopleTools-> Process Scheduler-> Processes.

2. Change the Search By field to "Process Name" and enter MY_PROCESS.

3. Click on the Process Definition Options tab.

4. Click the plus button to add a new row under the Process Groups section.

5. Type in CUSTOM (remember that this automatically adds it as a new Process Group).

6. Go to the appropriate Permission List and add the new Process Group.

Jobs

Jobs are simply collections of Processes that have been grouped together in order to run in association with each other. The Jobs component is also under *PeopleTools-> Process Scheduler* (or *PeopleTools-> Process Scheduler Manager-> Use-> Process Definitions* in earlier releases) and you follow the exact same procedure under the Jobs component Job Definition Options tab as you did on the Processes component in order to add the job to a Process Group.

6

Query Access Manager

PeopleSoft provides a powerful online query tool called Query Manager. Queries can be created and run online provided the proper access has been given to the tool and to the PeopleSoft tables.

Query Menu Access

The first step to setting up Query access is to grant the needed access to the Query Menu itself. You will generally have two types of Query users; those that need to build queries and those that need to only run pre-built queries. To accommodate this in versions 8.4 and above, PeopleSoft provides two separate component options for query, both under the Reporting Tools-> Query Menu. The first is the actual Query Manger Component that allows both build and view options for queries. The second is the Query Viewer Component, which can be given to users who only need to run queries, but not develop them.

Query Access Manager

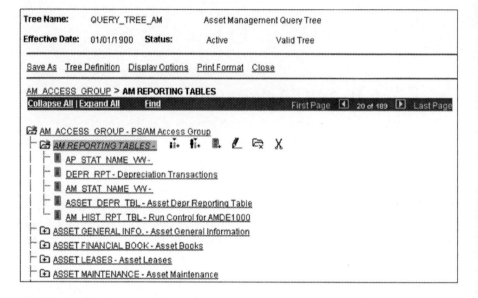

PeopleSoft delivers many Query Trees out of the box, which allow you to control specific tables users can access to query data from. These trees can be found under *PeopleTools-> Security-> Query Security-> Query Access Manager* in 8.4 and above, and under *PeopleTools-> Maintain Security-> Setup-> Query Access Group Manager* in earlier 8.x versions.

A tree is made up of Access Groups (denoted as folders in the tree structure itself) and Child Records (denoted with the icon that looks like a sheet of paper). Every tree must contain at least one high-level access group that serves as the root of the tree. Pay close attention to the names of the Access Groups themselves because it is the Access group, not the tree, which is added to the Permission List. Underneath this level you will find either other Access Groups or Child records, which are merely listings for tables within People-Soft that you are granting access to via the Access Group, or groups, in the hierarchical structure above it.

So let's say you need to add a new Access Group for the security team, which grants access to query against the PSAUTHITEM Table. You would follow these steps.

1. Open the Query Access Manager from either under *PeopleTools->Security-> Query Security-> Query Access Manager*, or from *People-Tools-> Maintain Security-> Setup-> Query Access Group Manager* depending on your PeopleTools version.

2. Click on the 'Create a New Tree' link.

3. Type in a name for your new tree, such as 'Security Tree'. You will also be required to give it a description, an effective date and a category, which you can choose from the ones PeopleSoft delivers. For this example we will choose 'Tools'.

4. Next you will be prompted for a Root Node for you new Tree. You may either use the search function to find an existing Access Group you wish to use, or you can simply type in an unused name to create a new one. We will create a new one called 'SEC_ACCESS_GROUP'.

5. The only formal thing you need to define on an Access Group Definition (which you are now prompted for) is a Description, although you may choose to fill in more details under the Definition section. We will simply describe ours as "Security Tables".

6. You will now see your tree with a single root node, SEC_ACCESS_GROUP. Click on the link for the Access Group Node and you will see a list of icons to the right denoting actions which you can perform related to your current level on the tree. Allow your mouse pointer to rest on each icon and after a moment a description of the option will appear. Here we have Insert Child Group, which would add another Access Group below your current level; Insert Child Record, which allows you insert a record into this Access Group; and Edit Data, which would allow you to edit the data for this Access Group that you just created. Click on the Insert Child Record button.

7. You can now select a record to add to the Access Group. For this example add PSAUTHITEM.

8. You can now select Save to save your Tree and Access Groups.

You can now add the Access Group to the proper Permission List, using the Access Group Permissions link on the Query Tab of a Permission List.

Common Query Access Issues

A user cannot see a table they wish to query from in Query Manager

This typically indicates that the user does not have access to the table via one of their Access Groups. Double-check that they have the proper Access Group on one of their Permission Lists and add the table to an Access Group if necessary.

A user cannot see a public query from the search screen in either Query Manager or Query Viewer

Once you have determined that the query does in fact exist, and is indeed a Public Query, then the user probably does not have access to all the tables being used in the query. If a user does not have access to all the tables involved in a query, the Search Screen itself will filter out the Query, so that it does not even appear in the list. Double-check that they have the proper Access Group on one of their Permission Lists and add the table to an Access Group if necessary.

7

Row Level Security

Row Level security provides a layer of Data security within the PeopleSoft system. Instead of securing the Page (and thereby the Record) a user has access to, Row Level security secures the actual rows of data within a Record that the user is allowed to see. For instance, let's say that you are the manager of Department X, which has 10 employees. You have access to the Job data via the Job Data component found under Administer Workforce. Row Level Security would be used to prevent you from accessing the job data for everyone in the company. It would do this by using a view for the search that only allows you to see the rows of data in the Job table for the employees in Department X, and not other departments.

This is just one example of how Row Level Security is used within the People-Soft system, but it works basically the same wherever it is implemented. You can access data within a certain table, via a certain Page and Component, but only the rows of data within that table that you have been set-up to see. Sounds great, huh? Let's look at some of the more common uses and set-ups within Financials and HRMS.

 Please note that the PeopleSoft system is highly complex and continually evolving. The next two sections describe two of the most common uses of Row Level Security, but are not all-inclusive. For further details of Row Level security options, please refer to the documentation for your specific modules.

Row Level Security in Finance

Row Security in Finance is mostly tied through the Primary Permission List. You can secure data based on various securable fields, which are customizable based on your needs.

Choosing Your Options

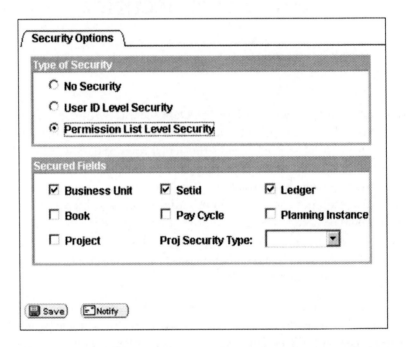

The first step toward Row Level security in Finance is to determine what (if any) level of Row Security you need. On the Security Options page (found under *Set Up Financials/Supply Chain-> Security*) you will find your options.

- No Security: No row level security is being used in the system.

- User ID Level Security: Row Level security is being implemented based individual User ID's.

- Permission List Level Security: Row Level security is being implemented based on Primary Permission Lists.

The number of users in your system will often drive your choice of Security Type. Understand that if you choose User ID Level Security, you will have to define your security access by each and every user, which can be extremely labor intensive to set-up and maintain. If you choose Permission List Level Security on the other hand, you will define the security options based on Permission Lists. You would then assign the Permission lists to a User as a Primary Permission List on the User Profile. Any changes would then be made to the Primary Permission List's settings not to each individual user affected. Keep in mind though that each user can only have one Primary Permission List assigned, so if your options are complex and very individualized, you may still need to use User ID Level Security.

Secured Fields

Here you select the key fields you want to base your Row Level restrictions on.

Business Unit	This field serves as a key for transaction data in the system.
Setid	This field serves as a key on setup type tables, such as setting up rules and accounting structure for the system.
Ledger	This field serves as the key for ledger balances.
Book	This field serves as a key to further delineate transactions under a Business Unit.
Pay Cycle	This field serves a key for Pay Cycle intervals.
Project	This field serves as a key for all Projects related data and can be defined either by choosing to setup based on a list or on a tree.

Setting Up Your Security Options

Under *Set Up Financials/Supply Chain-> Security* you will find the Pages you will use to define Row Level security for the secured field options you have chosen. You will generally see that for every Field you could choose to secure there are two menu options here for setting up the access, one that specifies by User ID and the other by Perm List. Be aware that the page for Projects is specially built and its appearance will change based on the Projects' security options you have chosen.

In addition you will find the *NVision Ledger Security* page. This page allows you to specify Business Units and Ledgers that may be used by nVision report users and writers, by User specifically instead of by Primary Permission List, even though that may be the main option chosen. This is necessary when nVision needed data may cross over ledger and business unit boundaries for which users may not otherwise be granted access.

Applying Your Row Level Security Options

Once you have done the configuration for your Row Level Security options, you must run a process to change the key field prompt tables to the views required for your options. Navigate to *Set Up Financials/Supply Chain-> Security-> Apply Security Setups*. This page controls the FIN9001 (Apply Security Setups) Process. Choose the correct parameters and then run it like any other process.

You can see a chart of the views that are being used based on the various security configurations by navigating to *Set Up Financials/Supply Chain-> Security-> Security View Names*. This page can be updated if you have special security needs and need to modify or create new views to accommodate your situation. Unless you are really sure about what you are doing it is recommended that you set the standard page security access for this page to Display Only and only refer to it as a reference for troubleshooting.

Row Level Security in HRMS

While the Row Level Security we discussed for Finance was mostly tied to the user through the Primary Permission List, most of the relevant Row Level Security in HRMS is tied through the Row Security permission list on the General Tab of the User Profile. Also be aware that while your main concern in Finance was probably to secure Business Units, the main concern of Row Level Security in HRMS is the securing of employee data based on Departments.

Building your Department Trees

Department trees provide the basic structure you will use to secure rows of employee data within your HRMS database. It is therefore very important that these are built correctly and maintained regularly. For this reason, it is recommended that someone in HR own the Department tree itself, since they are closest to the source of the data (new departments, transfers, new managers, etc…). That said, be very careful as an administrator when working with the Department Trees, as HR managers tend to carry big sticks.

To access Tree Manager navigate to *PeopleTools-> Tree Manager-> Use-> Tree Manager* (please not that this is the navigation for 8.x tools prior to 8.4). The default Department security is named DEPT_SECURITY and the SetID is Share, although you may choose to create one to operate with a different Setid, depending on your environment.

Tree Manager here works pretty much the same as discussed in terms of the Query Access Manager. The root level on this tree represents your company or organization. Below that you are adding departments in a hierarchical manner until you have built on organizational chart of your company's department structure. When you click the link on one of the department levels to either insert a child or a sibling node, you will be allowed to either choose an existing department that has been created or to create a new department on the fly by clicking *Add*.

Tie Data Permission Lists to your Trees

Once your Department Tree has been created, you will need to tie your Row Security Permission Lists to levels on the tree. To do this, navigate to *Define Business Rules-> Administer HR System-> Use-> Maintain Row Level Security*.

1) Choosing Your Permission Lists

The first thing you need to do here is select a permission list. These Permission Lists will need to be created just like any other permission list through the Maintain Security menu. You can name these in any way you choose, although the PeopleSoft standard is to generally to preface them with 'DP'. Depending on your organizational structure, you may find it useful to create a separate Permission for the manager of each department, such as DPDPT001 for Data Permission List for Department 001. Believe or not, this decision can be very important because it could cause you much confusion and grief in the future so try to choose a naming scheme that makes as much sense as possible for the people who will maintaining the tree in the future.

2) Adding Departments

Once you have selected your Permission List, you will be on the Data Security Profiles Page. Here you will add the Departments that this Permission List will have access to. You will need to provide the SetID for the Department Security Tree you are using and then enter the DeptID for the node you are choosing.

 Please note that since the Department Security Tree is hierarchical, that by adding an access to a department, you are automatically granting access to all the departments below that node as well. If you need to exclude the data from a particular 'sub-department' you will need to add that department separately to the list, and choose 'No Access" as the Access Code instead of the default of 'Read/Write'.

Change the Security Basis for the System

The final step to implementing Row Level Security in HR is to change all the search views controlling which data is accessed on various pages. Luckily you don't have to manually change each one, as PeopleSoft has delivered a process that takes care of it all for you. Please note that you only run this process when turning on Department Security system-wide, or when removing it from the system.

Navigate to *Define Business Rules-> Define General Options-> Process-> Change Row Security Basis*. This is a simple Run Control page, so you need to add a new Run Control if it is needed. Now you will choose the option for Department Security, to turn Department Security on, or the option of 'None', to turn Department Security off. Once you have made your selection press the Change Security button and check the Process Monitor to be certain the process completes without error. Now you are done!

8

Portal Structure

The use of the Portal in PeopleSoft version 8.4 adds a whole new wrinkle to security, but luckily it is mostly controlled in the background. Except for the troubleshooting of issues and periodic runs of the Portal Synch (PORTAL_CSS) process, you will usually not have to deal with the portal structure on a daily basis. For the occasions when you need to dive in though, here is a run-down of the basics. Again since most of the Structure and Content of the Portal is either controlled by developers or by PeopleSoft logic, you only want to make security corrections here as a last resort.

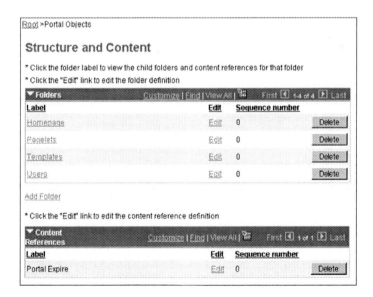

To see the basic Structure and Content of the Portal you should navigate to *PeopleTools-> Portal-> Structure & Content*. You will see the navigation point you at in terms of the Portal itself as a string of "breadcrumb" links at the top of the page so you can quickly reference where you are and move back as needed. Each level is made up of Folders and Content References. The folders represent another level or grouping (Structure) in the Portal while Content references are the actual page (or more precisely Component) links contained in the current level. Starting from the Root you will see that the structure reflects all the options you would see for the most part if you were navigating with "All Pages" type permissions.

Folders

By hitting the Edit link on a Folder you will be taken into a Component allowing you to access Folder Administration and Folder Security.

The Folder Administration page contains basic administration options for the folder, such as labeling, valid dates for the folder and other attributes. This page does not generally relate to security issues with a couple of exceptions. One problem can arise because of a valid date problem making a folder or link unavailable. The other problem may arise if the option to "Hide from portal navigation" has been selected, in which case you will never see the folder no matter how much access a Permission List may have.

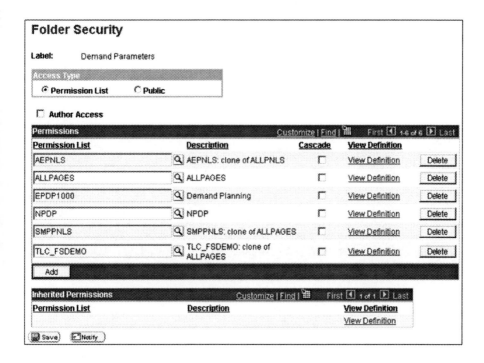

The Folder Security Page is very important. First you will see an option for Access Type, which sets whether you will control access by Permission Lists or whether you want to make the folder or page accessible publicly to everyone with access to the portal. The Permissions section shows the Permission Lists that have access to this Folder or page. Again these permission lists are added automatically when you hit save when assigning pages to a permission list. If they ever get out of sync, they can usually be fixed by running the PORTAL_CSS Application Engine process.

Keep in mind that access to the Folder in the Portal Structure does not mean that you have access to Content (Components) within the Folder. You merely have access to the Structure; Component and Page access are still controlled by Permission Lists.

Content References

You reach the *Content Ref Administration* Page by clicking the Edit link on the Content Reference. Again this represents Content (a Component) available at the current Folder Level of the Portal Structure. The administration page is similar to the Folder administration page and not something you will generally need to worry about in terms of security administration. The Component Parameters provide a convenient reference for the associated Menu.

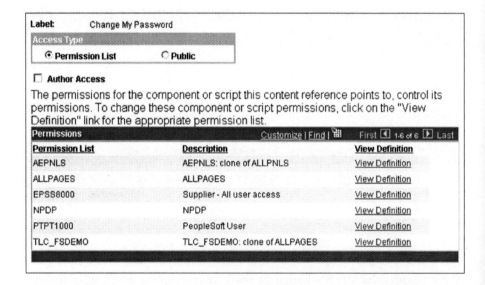

The Content Reference Security page is almost identical to the Folder Security page. The major difference is that you cannot add or remove Permission Lists associated with the page here. You can however click the View Definition link to edit the Permission List directly, which is the master for the Page Permissions.

Running Portal Synch Process

For various reasons, such as part of a migration procedure, you will need to run the PORTAL_CSS Application Engine Process. This process provides synchronization between the Portal Content and the traditional PeopleSoft Permission List based security. Before running this process, be sure to log in with an account attached to the 'Portal Administrator' Role.

Prior to 8.42

There are two possible ways to run the PORTAL_CSS Program. Before **version 8.42** you need to navigate to *PeopleTools-> Application Engine-> Request AE*. You will need to either add a new process request, choosing PORTAL_CSS as the Program, or simple select an existing request for it.

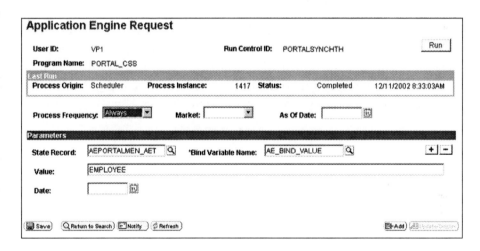

On the Application Engine Request page you need to set the options as shown above (Note that the Value used in Parameters depends on the Portal you are running the process for, such as EMPLOYEE, CUSTOMER or SUPPLIER). Next click Run.

Choose the option for "Portal Cref Security Sync" (a.k.a. PORTAL_CSS) so that it will be the actual program that runs in conjunction with the variable options you chose on the request page. Now click OK to launch the process.

To check the status of your job, navigate to *PeopleTools-> Process Scheduler-> Process Monitor*. This page will display by default Process Requests owned by your User ID for the last day. Hit refresh periodically until you see the Run Status reach Completed. The process can take around 10 minutes or more to run, depending how long it has been since it was last run.

After 8.42

On **version 8.42 or above** the process for running the Portal Synch has been greatly simplified. Navigate to *PeopleTools > Portal > Portal Security Sync*. Create a new run control or choose an existing one. From here choose the appropriate Portal name and select your options.

Update Content Ref Permissions: This is the basic Portal Synch option. It synchronizes Permissions with their appropriate Content References.

Update Folder Permissions: This option cleans up security on the actual folders themselves. Basically it removes all folder security (provided they have subfolders or content references within them) and then rebuilds their security based on the permission lists contained in the content references under that folder. This should clear up any of the 'Dangling Menus' issues discussed earlier.

Portal Security Synchronization

Run Control ID: DailySynch   Report Manager   Process Monitor   Run

*Portal Name: EMPLOYEE   🔍

☑ Update Content Ref Permissions
☑ Update Folder Permissions

Be aware that you will always find some sort of errors in the log for the Portal Synch runs. These consist of "Security Synchronization failed for..." errors. These are normal and should not cause alarm. If you are continually not getting the desired results, try running the process off-hours when users are not logged on, or retry the process logged in with VP1 or an equivalent ID.

Portal Registry Wizard

As a security administrator it will generally not be your responsibility to place menu items and pages on the Portal itself, but you should be aware of how developers go about doing this. You may also need to re-register a troublesome component after it has been migrated if the Content Reference is not showing up under the *Portal-> Structure & Content Menu.*

In Application Designer there is a Wizard that steps you through the process of registering your objects on the Portal to make them accessible. You can access the Portal Registration Wizard in one of two ways through Application Designer. First open the Menu Object that contains the Component you wish to register. Now select the component in the menu. You now can either choose *Tools-> Register Menu Item*, or right-click on the Component to choose it from the context menu there.

The initial screen gives you two options. The first allows you to use the wizard to add the component to the portal registry. The second allows you to add the component to a Permission List as well. By default both options are selected and it is generally useful to go ahead and use both.

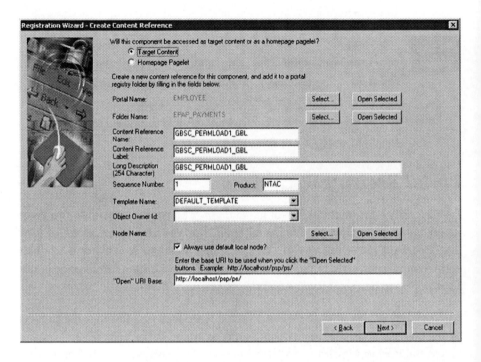

Select EMPLOYEE for the Portal Name. Next select the name of the Folder you want to place the Component in. You can find the name by checking through the Portal-Structure and Content menu online. The Content Reference Name will be generated for you, so simply leave it alone. The Content Reference label is the label displayed for the registry entry, and the Long description is what will show when you hover over the entry. Unless told otherwise just select 'Always use default local node?' under Node Name. The sequence number controls where the content reference will appear in the Folder. Use a number like 999 if you want to make it appear at the end.

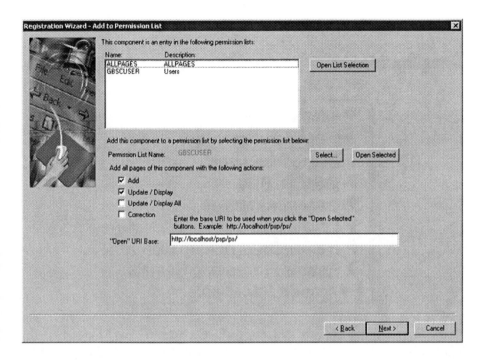

Simply select the proper security settings you want the component to be given in whichever permission list you choose to add it to. Notice that the options are simplified here. They cover all pages in the component and there is no Display Only option, so you may have to go into the permission lists online and make adjustments.

Now review the settings and hit finish.

Once this is done you will need to run the Portal Synch Process and then check to see if it the component is listed correctly with the proper security under the *Portal-> Structure & Content* menu. Once this is confirmed you may then need to run the Portal Synch one more time if it remains not visible within PIA.

Common Portal Issues

Dangling Menus

```
▼ Interface Transactions
  ▼ RMA Adjustments
  ▷ Billing Worksheet
  ▷ Maintain Bills
  ▷ Generate Invoices
  ▷ Locate Bills
  ▷ Review Billing Information
  ▷ Review Processing Results
▷ Accounts Receivable
```

You will sometimes run into situations where a user will see Menus (actually Folders in the Portal) that they are not supposed to see. Clicking on these folders will never show an actual Page link because there is no Page access granted. They do not hurt anything, but can be very distracting and confusing for the end user.

The first suggestion to try and correct this is to run the Portal Synch (PORTAL_CSS) process (discussed in next section). This may or may not clean up the problem. I have personally never had much success with it fixing this particular issue, but it is still suggested.

The second option is to go into the Permissions Page for the folder and manually delete the Permission List associated with the User that should not be there. This can be tricky because you need to trace back from the User ID to the Associated Role and then the Associated Permission Lists, of which there may be many to check. Ultimately patience and trial and error are your best bets here, though I suspect a good query could be written to hunt down all unnecessary references if it becomes a large problem.

Missing Access

Sometimes (especially when dealing with newly created Roles) you will have a situation where someone has Permission List access granted to a page, but still cannot see it. When they click the link they will go to a page that simply has the following error and nothing else (not even portal navigation menus):

You are not authorized for this page.
http://...

You should check the Content Reference security for the page and see if the proper Permission List is present. If it is not, then try making a minor change to the permission list (such as changing the text in the description) and then save the permission list again. Now check to see if it shows up correctly in the Content Reference security.

If the permission list is still not there you will need to run the Portal Synch (PORTAL_CSS) process, and if it still does not show up you may need to create a new version of the Permission List and use the new one instead.

Now for tricky part, even if the Permission List is listed properly in the Content reference security (whether you had to fix it or it was there to begin with) you may still have users that are unable to reach the page. This generally is an issue with the cache on the web server itself. By default this cache is set to refresh every 24 hours on the web server's CONFIGURATION.PROPER-TIES file. You can either wait it out, or bug your web administrator to dump the cache manually.

9

Security Migration & Back-Up

During a project you will need to migrate your work on security between databases. PeopleSoft delivers data mover scripts that allow you export your security (Users, Roles, Permission Lists, etc...) to a flat file, and then another script to import them into another database. These scripts can also be used to create a backup of your security set-up before making major changes in an environment, or just on a regular basis as a secondary flat-file backup.

Security Export

The Two Data Mover scripts you will use to export security are called SECURITYEXPORT.DMS in 8.4 and EXPOPR.DMS in releases prior to 8.4. These scripts are found in your PSHOME directory under the 'scripts' folder. Below are the steps you need to take to do the export.

1. Log in to the Data Mover Tool.

2. From within Data Mover choose *File-> Open* and browse to the *<PSHOME>\scripts* folder for the environment you wish to export the data from.

3. Select the *securityexport.dms* file or the *expopr.dms* if you are working with a tools release prior to 8.4, and click Open.

4. After the comments in the header of the file, you will find two lines similar to these:

    SET OUTPUT SECURITYEXPORT.DAT
    SET LOG SECURITYEXPORT.LOG

    These lines specify the filename and location for both your export flat file (SECURITYEXPORT.DAT) and your log file for the process (SECURITYEXPORT.LOG). I suggest that you rename these files to signify the environment and date, such as FS_DEMO_0609.DAT, and that you make it run to your local drive by changing it to C:\FS_DEMO_0609.DAT.

5. Once the file names have been changed, click *File-> Save*, or *File-> Save As* to save your file.

6. You can now perform the export by choosing *File-> Run Script* or by clicking the button on the toolbar that looks like a stoplight on 'green'.

7. You should see a message in the bottom pane of the Data Mover Tool informing you that the export completed successfully.

Security Import

The Two Data Mover scripts you will use to import security are called SECURITYIMPORT.DMS in 8.4 and IMPOPR.DMS in releases prior to 8.4. These scripts are found in your PSHOME directory under the 'scripts' folder. Below are the steps you need to take to do the import.

1. Log in to the Data Mover Tool.

2. From within Data Mover choose *File-> Open* and browse to the *<PSHOME>\scripts* folder for the environment you wish to export the data from.

3. Select the *securityimport.dms* file or the *impopr.dms* if you are working with a tools release prior to 8.4, and click Open.

4.   After the comments in the header of the file, you will find two lines similar to these:

SET INPUT SECURITYEXPORT.DAT
SET LOG SECURITYEXPORT.LOG

These lines specify the filename and location for both your import flat file (SECURITYEXPORT.DAT) and your log file for the process (SECURITYEXPORT.LOG). Enter the filename and path for your export file in the SET INPUT line, and choose the appropriate name and location for your log file.

5.   Once the file names have been changed, click *File-> Save*, or *File-> Save As* to save your file.

6.   You can now perform the export by choosing *File-> Run Script* or by clicking the button on the toolbar that looks like a stoplight on 'green'.

7.   You should see a message in the bottom pane of the Data Mover Tool informing you that the import completed successfully.

10

Definition Security

PeopleSoft Provides Definition security to add yet another layer of Application Designer security not found in the PeopleTools security options on a Permission List. Whereas the Permission List based security allows you secure *types* of objects with in Application Designer (such as Pages or Records), Definition Security allows you to secure *individual* objects (such as the menu MAINTAIN_SECURITY or the JOB record definition) while allowing normal access to other objects of that type.

Groups

From within Application Designer, choose *Go-> Definition Security*, or *Go-> PeopleTools-> Object Security* if you are in a tool-set prior to 8.4. Definition security is set-up using Groups. These groups are simply groupings of object definitions that you wish to secure in the same manner. PeopleSoft delivers a PeopleTools group that is a collection of all the PeopleTools related objects. To open existing groups *choose File-> Open-> Group*. To create a group from scratch, choose *File-> New Group*.

By default on a new or existing group, you will see a list that includes all the object types in a particular group. To see only a specific object type you simply change the value in the drop-down at the top, which will say 'All Objects'. You will notice that once you change the view to a specific type, the screen changes and opens up a second column area. The first column shows the object definitions currently included in the group. The second column shows those object definitions that are excluded from the group. Don't let the terminology confuse you here: 'excluded' simply means that the object definition is not a part of the current group.

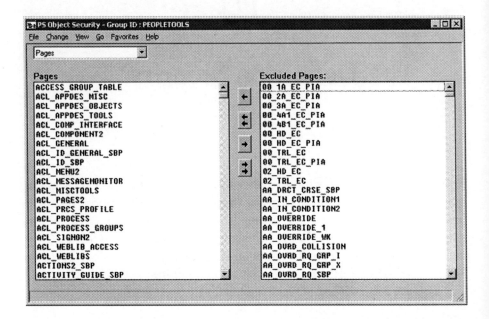

To add object definitions to the group simply highlight the desired object on the right and then click the single arrow button pointing to the left. To add all object definitions on the right to the current group, click the double arrow button pointing to the left. To remove object definitions from the group, simply follow the same procedures in reverse.

 Be aware that once an object definition has been placed in a group, it is automatically secured. This means that unless rights for the group are explicitly granted to a user via a Permission List, no one will be able to access this object in Application Designer.

Permission Lists

The next step in Object Security is to associate the group with a Permission List. To do this you first need to open the desired Permission List by choosing *File-> Open-> Permission List*. You may then choose from any Permission List that has been created already in the system through the normal Permission List creation process.

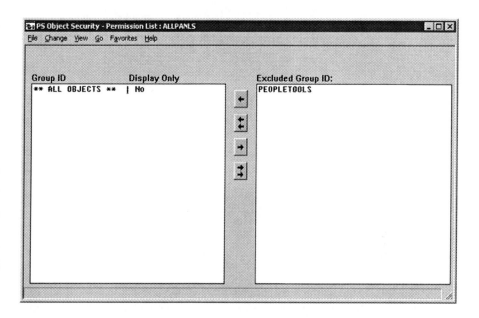

Once the Permission List detail is open, you will again see a left and right pane. The Left pane displays the groups and their corresponding access that have been tied to this permission list. The Excluded groups shown on the right pane are the groups whose objects definitions are not accessible through this Permission List. Note here that PeopleSoft delivers a dynamic group called 'ALL OBJECTS' which contains everything.

In the example on the screenshot, if you wished to add the PeopleTools group you would select it in the Right pane and then click the single arrow pointing to the left. Once it is in the left hand pane you must decide if it needs to be designated for full access or read only by changing the Display Only option. You change this by choosing Change-> Display Only from the menu. This brings up a Definition Security List dialog box. Here you simply highlight the Group Id's you wish to be read-only for the Permission List and click OK. To change it back you follow the same procedure and click to remove the highlighting and press OK.

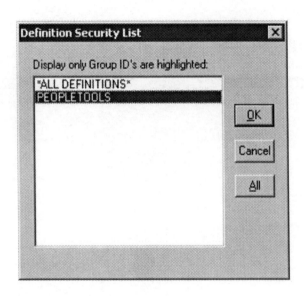

Tying Object Security to a User

As of at least PeopleTools 8.43 and 8.2, Definition security is assigned to a user through their Primary Permission List. This means that even though a user has access to a permission list, such as ALLPAGES, they do not automatically receive the Definition security assigned to that permission list. Definition security is only granted through the Primary Permission List assigned to the user on the General tab of the User Profile component. This means that these permissions cannot be assigned cumulatively (using a combination of Permission Lists), but must be assigned using only one per user via their Primary Permission List.

11

LDAP Authentication

PeopleSoft provides you with the option of integrating your PeopleSoft System with an approved LDAP based system. An LDAP based system provides a central Directory of Users and Passwords. This directory can be integrated to many systems such as email, PeopleSoft and other Enterprise-wide systems, to provide authentication for users. This means your users can use a single User ID and Password to login to multiple systems. This simplifies the maintenance of Users and passwords by centralizing it, and also makes it easier for users to remember their passwords since they are all the same, and not different based on the system. PeopleSoft currently supports integration with Microsoft Active Directory Services, Novell NDS and Netscape iPlanet.

How It Works

When you configure PeopleSoft to allow authentication through an LDAP compliant directory, you are basically telling it to try authenticating against the LDAP server if it fails to authenticate through the PeopleSoft system itself. Here is an example:

Say Rob's User ID is 'rjm01', and his PeopleSoft Password is 'J0eJ0e'. He also has an account on the Microsoft Active Directory server with same user name, but the password here is 'D@v1d'. If he attempts to login to PeopleSoft with 'rjm01' and the password of 'D@v1d', PeopleSoft will first try to authenticate him by checking the password entered against the Password on the PSO-PRDEFN table within PeopleSoft itself. Since the passwords do not match the login will fail. However with LDAP enabled, on the failure against the PeopleSoft password, it will then try to authenticate against the Microsoft Active Directory password. Since this password matches, Rob will then be allowed to pass into PeopleSoft as 'rjm01', since the LDAP server has been configured to be trusted for authentication.

Configuring LDAP in 8.4x

Configure Directory

The first step to setting up LDAP in 8.4x is to configure the Directory settings. Navigate to *PeopleTools-> Security-> Directory-> Configure Directory*. If this is a new Directory setup you should choose to *Add* a new **Directory ID**.

> Directory Setup

You next should enter a **Description** for your directory (so you can easily identify it) and then choose the **Directory Product** you are connecting to from the list PeopleSoft provides. If your directory is not listed (if it isn't Microsoft AD, Novell NBDS or iPlanet) then you can choose the option of Other LDAP Directory, but there are no guarantees that it will be supported.

Now come the specifics. You will need a **Default Connect DN** (*DN = distinguished name*) and **Password** to make the connection to the LDAP server. This ID will need to be setup by your LDAP administrator and given to you.

Under the **Server Name** section you will specify your **LDAP Server** using either its DNS name or its IP Address. You will then need to specify the Port (the standard port is 389) and an SSL port if there is a Secure Socket Layer being used. Note that you can configure multiple Servers in case any one of them is down, provided that they are all participating in the same directory service.

> Additional Connect DN's

On this page you may add **Additional Connect DN's** and their **Password** that may be needed for your Directory. These are usually more secure and used for their LDAP browse rights, which the Default Connect ID may not have.

> Schema Management

This page is only used if you are using the PeopleSoft Directory Interface, or PDI. This setup allows you to manage PeopleSoft-Specific Schema Extensions in your LDAP directory. This is not required for simply setting LDAP authentication and unless you have installed PDI, you will not have any Schema Extensions available on this page.

> Test Connectivity

Clicking on the tab for this page automatically shows you the details of a connection test to your LDAP directory. If you have configured everything correctly you should see a result of 'SUCCESS' for both the Bind and Search tests. If either of these fails, you need to review and redo your setup.

Cache Directory Schema

You next need to cache the directory schema from your LDAP server onto your PeopleSoft Database. This schema will provide you with the Object Classes and Attribute Types that you will need when creating your Authentication Map and User Profile Maps.

Navigate to *PeopleTools-> Security-> Directory-> Cache Directory Schema*. You will need to select your **Directory ID** for the settings you have created and then choose a **Server Name**. The Cache Schema process is actually an Application Engine program, so choose the server you would normally run an App Engine process on. Then click the *Cache Schema Now* button and check the Process Monitor to be certain it completes successfully.

Authentication Map

Navigate to *PeopleTools-> Security-> Directory-> Authentication Map*. You will need to create a new **Map Name** if one does not already exist.

> Directory Information

In this section you need to first specify the **Directory ID** you created for your LDAP configuration. Second you need to select **Anonymous Bind** if your directory all the authentication and user profile maintenance data to be accessed *anonymously*. You also need to check the **Use Secure Socket Layer Option** if you are using an SSL between PeopleSoft and LDAP.

If you are not using the **Anonymous Bind** option, you will need to specify a **Connect DN**. Your default Connect DN will be automatically entered in this field, but you can search for your additional Connect DN's by clicking the search button. You will then see a list of your additional Connect DN's if you chose to specify some earlier. If your default Connect ID did not have all the access needed for your setup, then you would select one of the additional ones here.

> List of Servers

This section allows you specify which LDAP servers the system should access for authentication, and the order in which they should be accessed. This list is pulled from the servers you specified in the Configure Directory step, and you should use the **SeqNum** field to specify the appropriate order needed for fail-over purposes.

> User Search Information

In the **Search Base** field you will enter the root level where PeopleSoft should begin its search for information on the users. Under **Scope Search** you will either choose *Sub*, which tells it to search the entire sub structure under your base, or *One*, which tells it to only search one level below your Search Base. You will never choose the *Base* option here.

Next you will choose the **Search Attribute**. The search attribute you choose will correspond to what the user enters for their ID when they login. This tells the system how to identify the corresponding user in LDAP. This will generally be some sort of user id in the LDAP system, such as *'uid'* or *'euid'*. Once this is chosen the **Search Filter** will display the string used to correlate the LDAP ID attribute to the PeopleSoft equivalent (%SignonUserId).

User Profile Map

A couple of very important things should be noted about LDAP and People-Soft. Even though LDAP can be configured to provide authentication into the PeopleSoft system, it is still the responsibility of PeopleSoft itself to assign rights to a user. This means that even if you are valid user in LDAP, People-Soft still needs information from the PSOPRDEFN table to present in its cache in order to assign the user rights associated with certain roles and permissions.

This is where the User Profile Map comes into play. Its settings can be used t automatically generate a PSOPRDEFN row for a new user who is valid in LDAP but does not exist yet in PeopleSoft. It can also be used to automatically update certain values at logon (such as an email address) which you may wish to 'master' from your LDAP directory, so changes are always made in LDAP not PeopleSoft to provide a single source for the data.

If used in conjunction with Role Membership rules, it is actually possible to never have to touch a user's information, via the User Profile Page, in PeopleSoft at all. The basic information needed to generate the PSOPRDEFN row comes from LDAP and a Query is used to determine which Roles should be cached for that user when they login.

> Mandatory User Properties

Navigate to *PeopleTools-> Security-> Directory-> User Profile Map*. If you have not already created a User Profile Map you will need to add one at this point. You will need to choose the **Authentication Map** that you created earlier and also fill in the **User ID Attribute**, which will correspond to the PeopleSoft OPRID.

A default **ID Type** will need to be selected. This corresponds to the ID type field on the ID page of the *User Profile* component. Be sure that if you select a value other than none, that you know the corresponding **ID Type Attribute** in the LDAP schema. So for instance if you chose the Employee ID Type you would need to choose an attribute on the LDAP server that contains the Employee ID for the ID Type Attribute.

You may also choose to set the **Use default Role** option. This would point to a Role (such as a Base User Role, discussed in Chapter 12) that all users in the system should be assigned to. Alternatively you could choose to enter a **Role Attribute** from LDAP that contains the name of the Role that should be assigned to each user. This is particularly helpful when you have a Base User Role for Employees that differs from a Base User Role for Customers on your Portal.

If you maintain a **Language Code** as an attribute in your LDAP schema you may wish to not select the **Use Default Language Code** option and instead either select a **LangCD Attribute** to specify the language code for the User. If you choose the Default Language Code option, then you should select the proper **Language Code** from the list for that field.

> Optional User Properties

The *Optional User Properties* allows you to choose other User Profile Attributes that you may want to populate from data being stored in LDAP. For each property chosen you will need to first select the **User Profile Property** you wish to populate. PeopleSoft allows you to choose the following:

- Currency Code
- Email Address
- Multi-Language Enabled
- Navigator Homepage Permission List
- Primary Permission List
- Process Profile Permission List
- Row Security Permission List
- Symbolic ID
- User Description
- User ID Alias

After choosing the **User Profile Property** you wish to populate, you need to decide if you will specify a default value or select a value from an LDAP attribute.

- To supply a default value, you need to select the **Use Constant Value** check box. You will then type your default value into the **Constant Value** field.

- To choose a value from LDAP instead, you need to enter the **Attribute Name** that corresponds to the value you want from LDAP.

Lastly you will choose whether or not you want this value to automatically update the User Profile every time the user logs in. If you choose the **Always**

Update option, the field will be updated at every login. If you do not choose this option, the field will only be populated when it is first created.

Role Membership Rules

The ability to dynamically assign Roles to a User is easily one of the most powerful features of the LDAP Interface. Properly creating these Rules though requires a good working knowledge of your LDAP schema, and the ability to maintain significant data in an attribute on your LDAP server that would allow you to decide the Roles required. For example, you might store Department ID's for users within LDAP. You could create a Rule that searches for a certain department, and then assigns a specialized Role for all users in that department.

The configuration of Role Membership Rules involves two steps:

1.   Creating the Rule itself via the *Role Policy* page, and…

2.   Tying the Rule to a Role using the *Dynamic Members* page on the Role component.

> Role Policy

Navigate to *PeopleTools-> Security-> Directory-> Role Membership Rules*. If this is a new Rule you should choose to Add. Enter a **Description** for your Rule and then choose the **User Profile Map** it should be associated with. In the **Search Base** field you should enter the container where you want your search to begin, and then choose the **Search Scope**.

You then build your Filter in much the same way you would define parameters in Query Manager. Use the combination of **Parentheses, Attribute, Operation, Value** and the **And/Or** field until you have created the filter you need. The **And/Or** field is highly significant, as selecting either 'AND' or 'OR' signifies another line in your Rule, while select 'END' signifies the end of your Rule, and selecting 'NONE' says that you re using this filter type.

The **Search Filter** field contains the values that apply to the DN search, which generally shows the directory object class for the container. An example of this would be "objectclass = person". Then lastly the **Directory Attribute** contains the attribute that will determine the members selected for the Role.

Signon PeopleCode

The logic needed for LDAP authentication is part of the Signon PeopleCode that fires off during a login to PIA. This is very important to remember because this is the reason that LDAP authentication only works online. It cannot work for Application Designer because the Signon PeopleCode is only called through PIA.

To turn on the Signon PeopleCode needed for LDAP, navigate to *People-Tools-> Security-> Security Objects->Signon PeopleCode*. This page allows you to select pre-existing sections of to run as part of the PeopleSoft Signon routine, and to specify the order in which they run. Notice that these rows list the **Record, Field Name, Event Name** and **Function Name** for each function available. To enable LDAP authentication, check the **Enabled** box on the row for the "LDAP_AUTHENTICATION" function on the "FUNCLIB_LDAP" record. Then also check the **Exec Auth Fail** option, which tells PeopleSoft to execute this code if the original authentication attempt (which goes against the native PeopleSoft password). Also if you are using the User Profile Map, you should also check the **Enabled** option on the "LDAP_PROFILESYNCH" function.

Also you should choose an ID to invoke the code as during sign on. You can choose to **Invoke as user signing in** but this will cause problems if it is a new user login, as they will not currently exist in the database. The better option is to choose **Invoke As** and then choose an existing **User ID** and **Password** to be used all the time. You need to be certain that this ID has access to the User Profile Component.

Once this is done and saved, you should shut down and restart all Application Servers for the database you are configuring.

 Be aware that if you are using LDAP authentication that the Signon PeopleCode function entitled "Password Controls" becomes irrelevant, since the passwords themselves are now being maintained by your LDAP system, not by PeopleSoft. It may also be a good idea to remove access to user's abilities to change their password within PeopleSoft in order to avoid confusion.

Configuring LDAP in 8.1x

For the most part, the configuration of LDAP in versions prior to 8.4 works in much the same way as 8.4. There are few less bells and whistles and therefore a few less steps.

Directory Authentication

Navigate to *PeopleTools-> Maintain Security-> Setup-> Directory Authentication*. The first step here is to check the **Use Directory Authentication** check box to tell PeopleSoft to use LDAP authentication. This option will automatically cause the LDAP_Authentication option to be selected on the *Signon PeopleCode* page.

Now you will enter the details. Under **Server name** you will enter either the DNS or IP Address for your LDAP server and then enter the correct **Port** number. You will then enter a **User DN** and **Password** that exists in LDAP with the needed rights to browse and read your entries. Next you will select your **Scope** (**base, one** or **sub**), your **Search Base**, which tells the system at what level to begin its search in LDAP, and your **Search Attribute**, which specifies what LDAP attribute you are matching to your PeopleSoft User ID.

User Profile Caching

Navigate to *PeopleTools-> Maintain Security-> Setup->User Profile Caching*. Here you will configure both **Mandatory User Properties** and **Optional User Properties**.

On the **Mandatory User Properties** page you will first need to pick a **User ID Attribute** that will specify the value to use as the UserID in PeopleSoft. Next you will choose a **Symbolic ID** to be used on all the new users and a **Role Name** that will serve as a default Base User Role for all the new users. You will now choose a default **ID Type** and the **ID Type Attribute** that provides the information (such as Employee ID) for the ID Type selected unless you choose a default of 'None'. You may also choose to **Use Default Language Code** in which case you will also need to specify the **Language Code** and **Language Code Attribute**.

On the **Optional User Properties** page you can choose from a list of available optional properties that can be automatically populated. For any that you choose you will also need to enter the **LDAP Attribute** that it corresponds to in the LDAP schema.

Directory Group Import

Prior to 8.4 the automatic assignment of Roles based on an attribute in LDAP is performed by using the Directory Group Import function. You 'import' a group of users based on a common attribute characteristic in LDAP. This attribute is what you use to distinguish groups needing a certain Role. You then assign the Directory Group to a Role and thereby complete the process of automatically tying an LDAP user to a Role in PeopleSoft.

> Configure the Import

Navigate to *PeopleTools-> Maintain Security-> Setup-> Directory Group Import*. If you do not already have a Map you are working with, you will need to do an Add and provide a **Map Name**. Next you must enter the **Server** (DNS or IP address of your LDAP server) and its **Port**. Then you must enter the **User DN** and **Password**. Then you must enter the **Search Base** and **Filter** and then choose a **Scope**. Finally you must choose the **Message** that will contain the results of the Import.

Now go to the **Attributes** page and fill in the **LDAP Attribute Name** that will correspond with each field on the Message you are using.

> Run the Import

Once you have completed the Directory Import Group Map, you will need to run the Import process itself. To do this, navigate to *PeopleTools-> Maintain Security-> Process-> Directory Group Import*. You will need to choose the name of your Directory Group Import Map to run and then click Run to submit it to the Process Scheduler.

> Assign the Directory Group to a Role

Now that you have created and imported your directory groups, you need to assign them to your Roles. To do this, navigate to *PeopleTools-> Maintain Security-> Use-> Roles* and select the Role you wish your Group to be assigned to. Next select the *Dynamic Members* page and turn on the check box for **Directory Rule Enabled**. Now you will need to click the **Assign Directory Groups** link, and here you will search for and select the Directory Group (or Groups) you wish to be assigned to this Role. Click OK and then Save the Role.

Signon PeopleCode

You also need to enable Signon PeopleCode for your LDAP options just like you would for version 8.4. To review you need to choose either **Invoke as user signing in** or choose **Invoke as** and then enter a **User ID** and **Password** with the proper access in LDAP. You must then be sure that the LDAP_AUTHENTICATION function has been enabled and is set to Execute if Authorization Fails. Also if you are synching the information from LDAP be certain the LDAP_PROFILESYNCH function is also enabled.

Once everything is complete you will need to restart all the Application Servers for your database.

12

Base User Profiles

The purpose of a Base User Profile is to provide a single Role that has the Permission needed by all users (or at least a large number of users) in a particular system. This Role can then be assigned to all users as they are created and any changes which need to be made to access for all users can be made via this single Role and its Permission Lists.

Page Access

For example, in most cases all system users will need access to the *My System Profile* menu that allows a user to change their email, password, currency code, etc...Since every user in the system needs access to this page it makes sense to put it in a single Permission List and Role instead of assigning it through Roles in various places and taking the chance that vital Permissions are missed. So you could create a Permission Lists and Role both with the name of BASE_USER, add access to the *My System Profile* Page and then be sure this new Role gets added to all users as they are created.

Component Interfaces & Web Libraries

In addition to pages, a Base User Profile is a good place to grant access to Web Libraries and Component Interfaces that all users need to be able to use for various processes. In fact, even though it violates the principle of least access, many places opt to add all Component Interfaces and Web Libraries to a Base User Permission List, rather than trying to keep up with which pieces are needed by which component. The access control then rests solely on a Users access to the Pages or Components in question through their PIA Navigation. As the number of Component Interfaces and Web Libraries that PeopleSoft delivers continues to increase, this becomes a more popular option.

 Be aware that when you grant access to a Web library or a Component Interface, that you are opening a backdoor which developers can use to manipulate the system. For instance, even though they do not have navigation access in PIA to a particular component, they could write a program against the Component Interface for that Component in order to access and manipulate data on the underlying table.

Sample Base Permission List Settings

The following settings provide an example of some things that might be included in a Base Permission List to grant basic system access and functionality.

Page Access

MENU: MAINTAIN_SECURITY
COMPONENT: USERMAINT_SELF
PAGE: USER_SELF_SERVICE

MENU: PROCESSMONITOR
COMPONENT: PROCESSMONITOR
PAGE: PMN_PRCSLIST

Web Libraries

WEBLIB_LEFTNAV
WEBLIB_MENU
WEBLIB_NAVMAIN
WEBLIB_TMEOUT

13

Password Controls

If you are managing your passwords within PeopleSoft itself, and not integrating to a third party LDAP tool for your authentication, then you may wish to take advantage of the Password Controls built into PeopleSoft. The options available vary a little between 8.4 and 8.1 and will be described separately.

Password Control Options in 8.4

Navigate to *PeopleTools-> Security-> User Profiles-> Password Controls*. In order to use the Password Controls at all, you must first choose the **Enable Signon PeopleCode** option, which will automatically select the "Password Controls" function on the Signon PeopleCode page.

Age

Your first set of options, refer to the age allowed for Passwords. You can choose **Password Never Expires** or choose an expiration period by choosing **Password Expires in** and then entering the number of days desired. If you are choosing to expire the passwords you will also want to choose whether to **Warn for** a particular number of days, or choose to **Do not warn of expiration** instead.

Account Lock

Here you choose the **Maximum Logon Attempts** allowed before the account is locked out. Choosing '0' means that the account will not be locked out due to erroneous attempts.

Miscellaneous

Check the **Allow password to match UserID** option only if you truly want passwords to be able to match user ids. In general this is a very risky practice and should be avoided.

Minimum Length

In the **Minimum Password Length** field enter the minimum allowed length for passwords in your system. The value of '0' states that there is no minimum length required, although the system itself still requires the password to not be blank.

Character Requirements

This section allows you to specify the Character Requirements of your passwords using the **Required Number of Specials** and **Required Number of Digits** fields. Again '0' implies no requirement. PeopleSoft considers all integers 0 thru 9 as Digits and the following characters are allowed as Specials:
! @ # $ % ^ & * () - _ = + \ |[ ] {} ; :/? . > <

Purge User Profiles

This option allows you to mark User Profiles to be purged from the system if they have not been used for a certain period of time. You simply set the **Purge**

User Profiles after field to the number of days appropriate for your system. Once again a value of '0' means the option is not in use.

 In addition to setting the Purge User Profiles option, the Application Engine program named PURGEOLDUSERS must be run on a regular basis in order for the delete to occur. This Program can be run directly from Application Engine Menu found under PeopleTools by choosing the Request AE component.

Password Control Options in 8.1x

Navigate to *PeopleTools-> Maintain Security-> Setup-> Password Controls*. In order to use the Password Controls at all, you must first choose the **Enable Signon PeopleCode** option, which will automatically select the "Password Controls" function on the Signon PeopleCode page.

Password Controls

☐ Enable Password Controls?

Age

◉ Password Never Expires

○ Password Expires in [0] Days

    ○ Warn for [0] Days

    ○ Do not warn of expiration

Minimum Length

[0] Minimum Password Length

Character Requirements

[0] Required Number of Specials

[0] Required Number of Digits

Account Lockout

[0] Maximum Logon Attempts

Miscellaneous

☐ Allow password to match UserID

(💾 Save)

Age

Your first set of options, refer to the age allowed for Passwords. You can choose **Password Never Expires** or choose an expiration period by choosing **Password Expires in** and then entering the number of days desired. If you are choosing to expire the passwords you will also want to choose whether to **Warn for** a particular number of days, or choose to **Do not warn of expiration** instead.

Account Lock

Here you choose the **Maximum Logon Attempts** allowed before the account is locked out. Choosing '0' means that the account will not be locked out due to erroneous attempts.

Miscellaneous

Check the **Allow password to match UserID** option only if you truly want passwords to be able to match user ids. In general this is a very risky practice and should be avoided.

Minimum Length

In the **Minimum Password Length** field enter the minimum allowed length for passwords in your system. The value of '0' states that there is no minimum length required, although the system itself still requires the password to not be blank.

Character Requirements

This section allows you to specify the Character Requirements of your passwords using the **Required Number of Specials** and **Required Number of Digits** fields. Again '0' implies no requirement. PeopleSoft considers all integers 0 thru 9 as Digits and the following characters are allowed as Specials:
! @ # $ % ^ & * () - _ = + \ |[ ] {} ; :/? . > <

14

Creating Dynamic Roles

The creation of dynamic Role assignments is a very useful part of the People-Soft Security Architecture, but it can also be a little frustrating when first encountered. You probably guessed by looking at the *Dynamic Members* page of the Role Component, that users can be tied to roles using a Query Rule which can be enabled and then the actual PeopleSoft Query selected right there on the page. The query itself should simply be built to select the User IDs that should belong to the Role based on some logic in the query, right? Unfortunately this is a trick question.

PeopleSoft has built in security within the PS Query tool that will automatically add "AND OPRID =", and then the current user's OPRID to all queries on tables that have OPRID as a key. Put plainly, this means that any query you build against the PSOPRDEFN table in order to select OPRID's will always only return your own OPRID, or simply return no information at all if you are not selected by the query.

The solution to this problem is to create a view within PeopleSoft that will contain the query logic needed to return your data, or at least a broad scope of data and criteria by which you may wish to choose your Role Users. Be certain this view contains OPRID but does not use it as a key. Once this is done then your PS Query selects OPRID from the View, not one of the delivered PS Tables.

Step 1: Create a View

Views are simply tables that are created from a query. They are given a table structure in the database itself, but the data contained in the table is dynamic and refreshed via the query it is based on. If you are unfamiliar with creating views in PeopleSoft, then you should consult with a PeopleSoft developer or DBA to help you create this in the best manner. A poorly built view can wreak havoc on database performance.

Again, be certain that OPRID is included in your view, but *is not* a key on the table.

Once the view is created, you will need to add it to a Query Access Group as described in Chapter 6.

Step 2: Create a Query

You will need to create your query in the PeopleSoft query tool. Again if you are unfamiliar with the creation of PS Queries you should refer to People-Books or seek the aid of a developer. The query itself needs to return the OPRID's for the users you want in the Role. If the logic in your view selects only the distinct users you need, then the PS query will simply select all the users in the view. If the view is a bit broader, then you need to build in more logic for selecting users from the view.

Step 3: Tie the Query to your Role

Go to the *Dynamic Members* page on the Role component (*PeopleTools-> Security-> Permissions & Roles-> Roles* in 8.4, or *PeopleTools-> Maintain Security-> Use-> Roles* in earlier releases). Select the checkbox for **Query Rule Enabled** and then select the query you created in the **Query** field under the **Query Rule** section.

Step 4: Test & Execute the Query Rule

To test your Query Rule, select a server to run the query on in the **Execute On Server** field, and then press the **Test Rule** button. If the data returned looks correct, then click the **Execute Rule** button to actually run the process that will put the users into the PSROLEUSER table.

APPENDIX A

PS 8.1 Security Tables

The following tables contain the majority of the PeopleSoft Data related to security for PeopleSoft 8.1x and 8.2x.

User Profiles

- PSOPRDEFN: Operator/User Profile Definitions
- PS_RTE_CNTL_RUSER: Contains Route Control Profiles used for Workflow, by Roleuser and Rolename.

User Profiles/Roles

- PSROLEUSER: Contains a separate line for each User/Role assignment combination
- PS_ROLEXLATOPR: Contains Roleuser info mostly related to workflow and email functions

Roles

- PSROLEDEFN: Role Definitions

- PSROLECANGRANT: Lists details of Roles allowed to grant other Roles, and which Roles, as part of PeopleSoft's distributed security model.

Roles/Classes

- PSROLECLASS: Contains a separate line for each Role/Permission List Assignment combination

Classes

- PSCLASSDEFN: Permission List Definitions
- PSAUTHSIGNON: Authorized Sign-On times for Permission Lists
- PSAUTHITEM: Contains individual lines for each Permission List/ Page combination, specifying all the menu and page item access granted to a permissions list as well as the Authorized actions and Display only status.
- PSAUTHPRCS: Contains individual lines for each Permission Lists/ Process group access combination.
- PSAUTHCUBE: Authorization for Permission lists and Data Cubes used for analysis
- PSAUTHBUSCOMP: Contains individual lines for each Permission List/Component Interface access and Method combination.
- PSAUTHCHNLMON: Contains individual lines for each Permission List/App Messaging Channel Access.
- PSPRCSPRFL: Contains the Process Profile settings for the Permission List used as the Process Profile for User Profiles

User Profiles/Classes

- PSOPRCLS: Contains the individual lines for each User/Permission List Combination

Access Profiles

- PSACCESSPRFL: This table contains the user-id and password used for the Access ID in the system. This table will generally contain a single entry; in UNT's case this is SYSADM1.

Tables populated by the Object Security tool

- PSOPROBJ: Contains all the setting for PeopleTools Object security tying Object Groups to Permission Lists.

Tables populated by the Query Security panels

- PS_SCRTY_QUERY: Contains the Query Profile Settings for each Permission List
- PS_SCRTY_ACC_GRP: Contains all combinations of Permission Lists and the query access groups assigned to them and their access level for each.

Tables populated by the Operator Alias panels

- PSOPRALIAS: Contains the Operator Alias data tied to Operator profile, such as Employee ID, etc...
- PSOPRALIASFIELD: Contains fields for holding data related to different types of Operator Aliases.
- PSOPRALIASTYPE: Contains the definitions for Operator Alias types.

Tables populated by mass change

- PS_MC_OPR_SECURITY: Contains Operator ID/Mass Change Template access combinations.

- PS_MC_OPRID: Records whether or not Operator ID's have permission to run Mass Change Definitions Online.

APPENDIX B

PS 8.4 Security Tables

The following tables contain the majority of the PeopleSoft Data related to security for PeopleSoft 8.4x.

ACCESS PROFILES

- PSACCESSPRFL: This table contains the user-id and password used for the Access ID in the system. This table will generally contain a single entry; in UNT's case this is SYSADM1.

USERS

- PSOPRDEFN: Operator/User Profile Definitions

- PSOPRALIAS: Contains the Operator Alias data tied to Operator profile, such as Employee ID, etc...

- PSROLEUSER: Contains a separate line for each User/Role assignment combination

- PSUSERATTR: User Attributes, such as Last Updated by & Time, Password Hint Question and Answer, etc...

- PSUSEREMAIL: Contains email addresses tied to Users and designates the Primary one for each in the system.

- PSUSERPRSNLOPTN: Contains Personal Options for Users.

- PS_ROLEXLATOPR: Contains Roleuser info mostly related to workflow and email functions
- PS_RTE_CNTL_RUSER: Contains Route Control Profiles used for Workflow, by Roleuser and Rolename.

ROLES

- PSROLEDEFN: Role Definitions
- PSROLEDEFNLANG: Contains Language codes (if any other than installed Language) associated with Roles
- PSROLECANGRANT: Lists details of Roles allowed to grant other Roles, and which Roles, as part of PeopleSoft's distributed security model.
- PSROLECLASS: Contains a separate line for each Role/Permission List Assignment combination

PERMISSION LISTS

- PSCLASSDEFN: Permission List Definitions
- PSAUTHBUSCOMP: Contains individual lines for each Permission List/Component Interface access and Method combination.
- PSAUTHCHNLMON: Contains individual lines for each Permission List/Component Interface access and Method combination.
- PSAUTHCUBE: Authorization for Permission lists and Data Cubes used for analysis
- PSAUTHITEM: Contains individual lines for each Permission List/ Page combination, specifying all the menu and page item access granted to a permissions list as well as the Authorized actions and Display only status.
- PSAUTHOPTN: Contains Personalization Options for Permission Lists

- PSAUTHPRCS: Contains individual lines for each Permission Lists/ Process group access combination.

- PSAUTHSIGNON: Authorized Sign-On times for Permission Lists

- PSPRCSPRFL: Contains the Process Profile settings for the Permission List used as the Process Profile for User Profiles

- PS_MC_OPR_SECURITY: Contains Operator ID/Mass Change Template access combinations.

- PS_MC_OPRID: Records whether or not Operator ID's have permission to run Mass Change Definitions Online.

- PS_SCRTY_ACC_GRP: Contains all combinations of Permission Lists and the query access groups assigned to them, and their access level for each

- PS_SCRTY_QUERY: Contains the Query Profile Settings for each Permission List

DEFINITION SECURITY

- PSOBJGROUP: Contains Object Group Definitions and entries

- PSOPROBJ: Contains the settings for PeopleTools Object security tying Object Groups to Permission Lists.

PERSONALIZATIONS

- PSUSEROPTNDEFN: User Option Definitions

- PSUSEROPTNLANG: Language Code related to User Options and Categories

- PSOPTNCATGRPLNG: Language Code related to Option Category Groups

- PSOPTNCATGRPTBL: Option Category Group Definitions

- PSOPTNCATTBL: Option Category Definitions

- PSOPTNCATLANG: Language code related to Option Category Definitions

SECURITY OPTIONS

- PSSECOPTIONS: System-wide security options, such as password related settings.

SECURITY LINKS

- PSUSEROTHER: Custom Defined links for User Profiles—Links
- PSUSERSELFOTHER: Custom Defined links for My Profile—Other Security Links
- PSROLEOTHER: Custom Defined links for Roles—Links
- PSPERMLISTOTHER: Custom Defined links for Permission Lists—Links

USER ID TYPES

- PSOPRALIASTYPE: Contains the definitions for Operator Alias types.
- PSOPRALIASFIELD: Contains fields for holding data related to different types of Operator Aliases.

DELETE USER BYPASS TABLE

- PS_BYPASS_TABLE: Defines Records to be bypassed during user delete process

FORGOT EMAIL TEXT

- PSPSWDEMAIL: Defines text for forgotten password email text

PASSWORD HINTS

- PSPSWDHINT: Defines text for password hint email

ACCESS LOGS

- PSACCESSLOG: Shows user login times as well as the LOGIPAD-DRESS field which will show you where the login occurred from

SIGNON PEOPLECODE

- PSSIGNONPPC: Contains references for Sign-On PeopleCode to be executed at sign-in, its order, etc…

APPENDIX C

Useful Security Queries

Please note that the following queries were written specifically for use in Oracle, but should function with minimal modifications against SQL Server as well. These by no means cover ever situation you will need to be able to query for security purposes within PeopleSoft, but they will give you a good place start. Also remember that there are delivered Security Queries within PeopleSoft in Version 8.4 and above, which run the Query Manager in PIA. These are found on many components themselves (such as User Profiles and Permission Lists) and can also be access by navigating to *PeopleTools-> Security-> Review Security Information.*

Users with a Particular Role

This query will show you all the users assigned to a specified Role. Replace **ROLE1** with the appropriate Role Name for your query.

```
SELECT ROLEUSER, ROLENAME
FROM PSROLEUSER
WHERE ROLENAME = 'ROLE1'
ORDER BY ROLEUSER
```

Users with a Particular Permission List

This query will show you all users connected to a particular Permission List. Replace **PERM1** with the appropriate Permission List Name for your query.

```
SELECT OPRID, OPRCLASS
FROM PSOPRCLS
WHERE OPRCLASS = 'PERM1'
ORDER BY OPRID
```

Users with a Particular Primary Permission List

This query will show you all users who have a specific Permission List set as their Primary Permission List. Replace **PERM1** with the appropriate Primary Permission List Name for your query.

```
SELECT OPRID, OPRCLASS
FROM PSOPRDEFN
WHERE OPRCLASS = 'PERM1'
ORDER BY OPRID
```

Users with a Particular Row Security Permission List

This query will show you all users who have a specific Permission List set as their Row Security Permission List. Replace **PERM1** with the appropriate Row Security Permission List Name for your query.

```
SELECT OPRID, ROWSECCLASS
FROM PSOPRDEFN
WHERE ROWSECCLASS = 'PERM1'
ORDER BY OPRID
```

Users, Role & Class with Access to a Particular Page

This query selects the users and their relevant Roles and Permissions, which are granting access to a particular page. The query also takes into account that the user is active and the page permissions are not Display Only.

Replace **PAGE1** with the appropriate Page Name for your query.

```
SELECT    B.ROLEUSER,    C.OPRDEFNDESC,    A.ROLENAME,
A.CLASSID
FROM PSROLECLASS A, PSROLEUSER B, PSOPRDEFN C
WHERE B.ROLENAME = A.ROLENAME
AND B.ROLEUSER = C.OPRID
AND C.ACCTLOCK = 0
AND A.CLASSID IN
(SELECT DISTINCT CLASSID
FROM PSAUTHITEM
WHERE PNLITEMNAME = 'PAGE1'
AND DISPLAYONLY = 0)
ORDER BY B.ROLEUSER
```

Roles & Class with Access to a Particular Page

This query shows you all the Roles and the relevant Permission List, which grant access to a particular page. Replace **PAGE1** with the appropriate Page Name for your query.

```
SELECT A.ROLENAME, A.CLASSID
FROM PSROLECLASS A, PSROLEDEFN B
WHERE A.CLASSID IN
(SELECT DISTINCT CLASSID
FROM PSAUTHITEM
WHERE PNLITEMNAME = 'PAGE1')
AND A.ROLENAME = B.ROLENAME
ORDER BY A.ROLENAME
```

Permission Lists & Details with Access to a Particular Page

This query shows you the full details for Permission Lists tied to a particular Page. Replace **PAGE1** with the appropriate Page Name for your query.

SELECT * FROM PSAUTHITEM
WHERE PNLITEMNAME = 'PAGE1'
ORDER BY CLASSID

Roles Assigned to a Particular User

This query shows you all the Roles assigned to a particular User. Replace **USER1** with the appropriate username for your query.

SELECT ROLEUSER, ROLENAME
FROM PSROLEUSER
WHERE ROLEUSER = 'USER1'
ORDER BY ROLENAME

Permission Lists Assigned to a Particular User

This query shows you all the Permission Lists assigned to a particular User. Replace **USER1** with the appropriate username for your query.

SELECT OPRID, OPRCLASS
FROM PSOPRCLS
WHERE OPRID = 'USER1'
ORDER BY OPRCLASS

Roles & Permission Lists Assigned to a Particular User

This query shows all the Roles and Permission Lists assigned to a particular User. Replace **USER1** with the appropriate username for your query.

```
SELECT A.ROLEUSER, A.ROLENAME, B.CLASSID
FROM PSROLEUSER A, PSROLECLASS B
WHERE A.ROLEUSER = 'USER1'
AND A.ROLENAME = B.ROLENAME
```

Permission Lists Assigned to a Particular Role

This query shows all the Permission Lists assigned to a particular Role. Replace **ROLE1** with the appropriate Role Name for your query.

```
SELECT * FROM PSROLECLASS
WHERE ROLENAME = 'ROLE1'
ORDER BY CLASSID
```

All Pages Accessible by a User

This query shows all the pages and details accessible by a particular User. Replace **USER1** with the appropriate username for your query.

```
SELECT A.ROLEUSER, A.ROLENAME, B.CLASSID,
C.MENUNAME, C.BARNAME, C.BARITEMNAME,
C.PNLITEMNAME, C.DISPLAYONLY, C.AUTHORIZEDACTIONS
FROM PSROLEUSER A, PSROLECLASS B, PSAUTHITEM C
WHERE A.ROLEUSER = 'USER1'
AND A.ROLENAME = B.ROLENAME
AND B.CLASSID = C.CLASSID
ORDER BY A.ROLENAME, B.CLASSID,
C.MENUNAME, C.BARITEMNAME, C.PNLITEMNAME
```

All Pages Accessible by a Role

This query shows all the Pages and details accessible by a particular Role. Replace **ROLE1** with the appropriate Role Name for your query

```
SELECT DISTINCT A.ROLENAME, B.CLASSID,
C.MENUNAME, C.BARNAME, C.BARITEMNAME,
C.PNLITEMNAME, C.DISPLAYONLY, C.AUTHORIZEDACTIONS
```

```
FROM PSROLEUSER A, PSROLECLASS B, PSAUTHITEM C
WHERE A.ROLENAME = 'ROLE1'
AND A.ROLENAME = B.ROLENAME
AND B.CLASSID = C.CLASSID
ORDER BY B.CLASSID,
C.MENUNAME, C.BARITEMNAME, C.PNLITEMNAME
```

All Pages Accessible by a Permission List

This query shows all the pages and details accessible by a particular Permission List. Replace **PERM1** with the appropriate Row Security Permission List Name for your query.

```
SELECT * FROM PSAUTHITEM
WHERE CLASSID = 'PERM1'
ORDER BY MENUNAME, BARITEMNAME, PNLITEMNAME
```

All Users with Access to Maintain Security

This query allows you to check on all the users in an environment that have access to the Maintain Security Pages. This query excludes the User Self Service and Password Change pages that most users do have access to.

```
SELECT B.ROLEUSER, C.OPRDEFNDESC,
A.ROLENAME, A.CLASSID
FROM PSROLECLASS A, PSROLEUSER B, PSOPRDEFN C
WHERE B.ROLENAME = A.ROLENAME
AND B.ROLEUSER = C.OPRID
AND C.ACCTLOCK = 0
AND A.CLASSID IN
(SELECT DISTINCT CLASSID
FROM PSAUTHITEM
WHERE MENUNAME LIKE 'MAINTAIN_SECURITY%'
AND PNLITEMNAME NOT IN
('CHANGE_PASSWORD', 'USER_SELF_SERVICE')
AND DISPLAYONLY = 0)
ORDER BY ROLENAME, ROLEUSER
```

All Users with Access to Application Designer

This query will return all *active* users with *non display-only* access to Application Designer.

```
SELECT DISTINCT A.OPRID, B.OPRDEFNDESC
FROM PSOPRCLS A, PSOPRDEFN B
WHERE A.OPRID = B.OPRID
AND B.ACCTLOCK = 0
AND A.OPRCLASS IN
(SELECT DISTINCT CLASSID
FROM PSAUTHITEM
WHERE MENUNAME LIKE 'APPLICATION_DESIGNER%'
AND DISPLAYONLY = 0)
```

APPENDIX D

Authorized Actions Codes on PSAUTHITEM

On the PSAUTHITEM you have a field that denotes whether or not access to a page is Display Only and then that is followed by a field with a numeric code that denotes the Authorized Actions given for the particular page access. This table shows the possible action combinations for *Page-based* access and the corresponding values. Please note that you may find some other values for *Tools-based* access (such as access given to Application Designer through the PeopleTools tab of a Permission List) and they differ in their use based on the particular tool in question.

Authorized Actions Code	Means...
1	Add
2	Update/Display
3	Add + Update/Display
4	Update/Display All
5	Add + Update/Display All
6	Update/Display + Update/Display All
7	Add + Update/Display + Update/Display All
8	Correction

Authorized Actions Code	Means...
9	Add + Correction
10	Update/Display + Correction
11	Add + Update/Display + Correction
12	Update/Display All + Correction
13	Add + Update/Display All + Correction
14	Update/Display + Update/Display All + Correction
15	Add + Update/Display + Update/Display All + Correction

APPENDIX E

Special PeopleSoft Roles

PeopleSoft delivers some special roles that allow users to perform various tasks they could not otherwise. These Roles do not grant access through their Permission Lists, but instead are hard-coded within PeopleCode to see if the User belongs to the Role. If the system verifies the User is a part of the special Role, then special access is granted.

ProcessSchedulerAdmin

The ProcessSchedulerAdmin Role can be given to a user to allow them to view all processes through the Process Monitor, regardless of who submitted them. They can also see the details on these jobs, as well as Stop, Cancel and Restart these processes.

ReportDistAdmin

The ReportDistAdmin Role allows a user to view all reports within the Report Manager regardless of the user. They can also use this access to delete reports from the Report Manager and to update distribution list and expiration for any report.

ReportSuperUser

The ReportSuperUser Role allows users to delete their own reports from Report Manager. They can also update the distribution list and expiration on any report that they have access to. It does not however grant the full rights to all reports like the ReportDistAdmin Role.

Portal Administrator

In order to run the Portal Security Synchronization Process (PORTAL_CSS) the user must belong to the Portal Administrator or the PeopleSoft Administrator role.

0-595-32440-1

Lightning Source UK Ltd.
Milton Keynes UK
01 February 2010

149404UK00002B/145/A